THIRD EDITION

SUMMIT 1

WORKBOOK

JOAN SASLOW
ALLEN ASCHER

Summit: English for Today's World   Level 1, Third Edition
Workbook

Copyright © 2017 by Pearson Education, Inc.

Pearson, 221 River Street, Hoboken, NJ 07030

Staff credits: The people who made up the *Summit* team representing editorial, production, design, manufacturing, and marketing are Pietro Alongi, Rhea Banker, Peter Benson, Stephanie Bullard, Jennifer Castro, Tracey Munz Cataldo, Rosa Chapinal, Aerin Csigay, Dave Dickey, Gina DiLillo, Christopher Leonowicz, Laurie Neaman, Alison Pei, Sherri Pemberton, Jennifer Raspiller, Mary Rich, Courtney Steers, Katherine Sullivan, and Paula Van Ells.

Cover credit: Tonis Pan/Shutterstock
Text composition: ElectraGraphics, Inc.

Photo credits: Page 1 (bottom): Felix Mizioznikov/Fotolia; 1 (bottom center): Ajr images/Fotolia; 1 (top): Jaimie Duplass/Fotolia; 1 (top, center): Vladimir Wrangel/Shutterstock; 3 (top): Andy Dean/Fotolia; 6: Ead72/ Fotolia; 7: Mirceait/Fotolia; 8: Zinkevych/Fotolia; 14 (bottom): Nanette Grebe/Shutterstock; 14 (top): Drx/ Fotolia; 18: Michael Jung/Fotolia; 19: Sueddeutsche Zeitung/Alamy Stock Photo; 26: WavebreakMediaMicro/ Fotolia; 31: Khoroshunova Olga/Shutterstock; 32: Mike Goldwater/Alamy Stock Photo; 36 (bottom, center, left): Heritage Image Partnership Ltd/Alamy Stock Photo; 36 (bottom, center, right): Dariazu/Fotolia; 36 (bottom, left): Racorn/123RF; 36 (bottom, right): Artranq/Fotolia; 36 (top, center, left): Pikselstock/Fotolia; 36 (top, center, right): Ajr Images/Fotolia; 36 (top, left): Looking2thesky/Fotolia; 36 (top, right): XiXinXing/Shutterstock; 37 (left): Viorel Sima/Fotolia; 37 (middle): Maxim Ahner/Shutterstock; 37 (middle, center): Iko/Fotolia; 37 (right): Kim/Fotolia; 37 (top, center, left): Boomeart/Fotolia; 37 (top, center, right): Nyul/Fotolia; 38: Monkey Business Images/Shutterstock; 39: Anamejia18/Fotolia; 41: BillionPhotos.com/Fotolia; 48: Ekaterina Elagina/ Fotolia; 50: Bildagentur Zoonar GmbH/Shutterstock; 51: Michele Gran/Global Volunteers; 55 (bottom, left): Eric Isselee/Shutterstock; 55 (bottom, right): Givaga/Shutterstock; 55 (center): Eric Isselee/Shutterstock; 55 (center, left): Flib/123RF; 55 (center, right): Tsekhmister/Shutterstock; 55 (top, center): Anankkml/Fotolia; 55 (top, left): Cheri131/Fotolia; 55 (top, right): Alexander Ishchenko/Shutterstock; 59: Fotolia; 60 (bottom, left): Kirsten Wahlquist/Shutterstock; 60 (bottom, right): Cheryl Davis/Fotolia; 60 (center): Peterralph/Fotolia; 60 (top, center): Tratong/Shutterstock; 60 (top, left): Cheryl Davis/Fotolia; 60 (top, right): Alexei Tm/Fotolia; 62: Gi0572/ Fotolia; 67 (bottom): Kurhan/Fotolia; 67 (bottom, center): PT Images/Shutterstock; 67 (top): Felix Mizioznikov/ Shutterstock; 67 (top, center): Rido/Fotolia; 68 (bottom, left): Pathdoc/Fotolia; 68 (bottom, right): Catherine Murray/Fotolia; 68 (top, left): Dglimages/Fotolia; 68 (top, right): Arek Malang/Shutterstock; 69: Delphotostock/ Fotolia; 71: Minerva Studio/Fotolia; 72: Rocketclips/Fotolia; 79: Phattana/Fotolia; 84: Sergey Chirkov/Fotolia; 85: Xalanx/Fotolia; 91 (bottom): Pathdoc/Shutterstock; 91 (bottom, center): Piotr Marcinski/Fotolia; 91 (center): WavebreakmediaMicro/Fotolia; 91 (middle, center): Phovoir/Shutterstock; 91 (top): Bruno135_406/Fotolia; 91 (top, center): Carlos Caetano/Fotolia; 93: Mary Evans Picture Library/Alamy Stock Photo; 98: Kurapatka/Fotolia; 100 (bottom, left): Dwayne Foong/Fotolia; 100 (bottom, right): Asier Romero/Fotolia; 100 (center, left): Michael Spring/Fotolia; 100 (center, right): Siarhei Zapatylak/Fotolia; 100 (top, left): Elena Elisseeva/Shutterstock; 100 (top, right): Innovated Captures/Fotolia; 101: Mat Hayward/Fotolia.

Illustration Credits: Leanne Franson, p. 3, 21, 27, 89; ElectraGraphics, Inc. p. 57–58

Printed in the United States of America

ISBN-10: 0-13-449958-1
ISBN-13: 978-0-13449958-1
2 17

Contents

1 For each situation, write a possible response from an optimist, a pessimist, and a realist.

1.

Did you see the email from our boss? She wants everyone to meet in the conference room at 4:00. I wonder what's going on.

a. optimist: _____

_____

b. pessimist: _____

_____

c. realist: _____

_____

2.

Your mother wants you to call her. She says it's really important.

a. optimist: _____

_____

b. pessimist: _____

_____

c. realist: _____

_____

3.

I just read an article about the Zika virus. They say it's likely to spread to our city soon.

a. optimist: _____

_____

b. pessimist: _____

_____

c. realist: _____

_____

4.

The weather report says there's a hurricane moving up the coast. What do you think we should do?

a. optimist: _____

_____

b. pessimist: _____

_____

c. realist: _____

_____

2 Complete the conversations with expressions from the box.

better safe than sorry	what are you going to do
have started getting to me	you've got to roll with the punches
it's just a matter of time	you're just a sitting duck

1. **A:** Did you hear that the flu is going around Sophie's school?

   B: Yes. I guess _____ before someone in our family comes down with it.

2. **A:** Did you get the raise you asked for?

   B: No. But _____? I'll try again in six months.

3. **A:** All the news stories about crazy weather events _____.

   B: I know. But I think you just have to live your life and try not to worry.

4. **A:** I didn't get the job I really wanted.

   B: Well, _____—keep applying, and I know you'll find a good job eventually.

5. **A:** With all the stories about terrorism in the news, I don't want to go anyplace that has crowds.
   I think _____.

   B: I know it's scary, but try not to overreact.

6. **A:** Did you lock the car?

   B: Yes. _____, right?

LESSON 1

3 Match the vocabulary words with their definitions. Write the letter on the line.

_____ 1. easygoing   **a.** unwilling to talk proudly about yourself

_____ 2. hardworking   **b.** able to be trusted or depended on

_____ 3. considerate   **c.** not easily worried or annoyed

_____ 4. modest   **d.** saying what you mean, not joking or pretending

_____ 5. outgoing   **e.** wanting to meet and talk to new people

_____ 6. trustworthy   **f.** working seriously with a lot of effort

_____ 7. serious   **g.** liking to talk a lot

_____ 8. talkative   **h.** thinking and caring about other people

4 **Complete the conversation. Write the letter on the line.**

A: How would you describe your sister?

B: _____
      1.

A: I guess that makes sense. You are pretty talkative…

B: _____
      2.

A: Me? Hmm. Hardworking… serious.

B: _____
      3.

A: Well, I suppose it's possible to be both.

B: _____
      4.

a. Yes, I suppose you're right.

b. I know. What about you—how would you describe yourself?

c. Well, she's a lot like me—pretty outgoing, I guess.

d. Really? I see you as friendly.

5 **Read the descriptions of Type A and Type B personalities. Then answer the questions.**

TYPE A

An outgoing, impatient, and sometimes rude personality. People with Type A personalities work hard to succeed and to get what they want. They are busy, often stressed out, and don't like to wait. They eat, talk, walk, and drive fast. They might seem unfriendly and difficult to get along with.

TYPE B

The opposite of Type A personality. The Type B personality is easygoing, modest, and friendly. People with Type B personalities are able to relax and have fun. They live a more balanced life.

1. Name someone you know who has a Type A personality. _____

2. What is this person like? Write three examples to support your opinion.

   _____

   _____

   _____

3. Describe your own personality. Are you more like a Type A or a Type B personality?

   _____

   _____

6 What qualities would you like the people in your life to have? Complete each sentence with two adjectives from the box. Try to use as many adjectives as you can.

considerate	fun	independent	modest	punctual	smart
easygoing	funny	intelligent	outgoing	serious	talkative
friendly	hardworking	interesting	polite	silly	trustworthy

1. I would like a boss who's _____.

2. I would like co-workers who are _____.

3. I would like a spouse who's _____.

4. I would like classmates who are _____.

5. I would like friends who are _____.

6. I would like neighbors who are _____.

7. I would like a teacher who's _____.

8. I would like to be more _____.

7 Complete each sentence with the gerund or infinitive form of the verb.

1. _____ hard is important in this company.
(work)

2. Amy volunteered _____ at the shelter after the storm.
(help)

3. Shawna's dream is _____ a doctor someday.
(be)

4. Roger apologized for _____ late.
(arrive)

5. Is that book short enough _____ in one night?
(read)

6. It's important _____ yourself some time to relax every day.
(give)

7. We considered _____ to California for our vacation.
(go)

8. We got to the exhibit early _____ the crowds.
(avoid)

9. It's too hot _____ soccer. Let's just go for a walk instead.
(play)

8 Complete the sentences about yourself. Use gerunds or infinitives and your own ideas.

1. I remember _____ when I was young.

2. I think it's exciting _____.

3. I can't wait _____.

4. I'm opposed to _____.

5. I would like _____ some day.

6. I would like to read a book about _____.

7. I am studying English _____.

8. I'm not quite wealthy enough _____.

9. _____ is my favorite form of exercise.

10. I avoid _____ if I can.

LESSON 2

9 Write a definition for each word or phrase.

Name	Definitions
a pain in the neck	
a people person	
a sweetheart	
a team player	
a tyrant	
a workaholic	

10 Rewrite each sentence in the active voice. Use the subject in parentheses.

1. The students were reminded to attend the meeting after school.

   (the teacher) _The teacher reminded the students to attend the meeting after school._

2. We were invited to go on a tour of the museum.

   (the director) _____

3. I was persuaded to donate money to the charity.

   (the ad) _____

4. Janice was hired to supervise the project.

   (the CEO) _____

5. The tourists were advised not to travel without the group.

   (the guide) _____

11 Complete the sentences, using your own ideas.

1. I taught _____my son_____ to _____knit_____.

2. I encourage _____ to _____.

3. I'd like _____ to _____.

4. I told _____ to _____.

5. I asked _____ not to _____.

6. I'll teach _____ to _____.

12 **CHALLENGE** Create sentences, using one word or phrase from each column. You can combine words several ways. Be sure to use a correct form of the verb in column 2 and the infinitive form of the verb in column 4.

1	2	3	4
Tahlia	encourage	her daughter	study hard
Julie	advise	Narisa	eat more fruit
The doctor	order	us	make dinner
Mark	teach	Terry	leave
We	pay	our neighbor	mow the lawn
The guard	would like	you	play the violin

1. _Tahlia would like you to make dinner._

2. _____

3. _____

4. _____

5. _____

6. _____

LESSON 3

13 **Answer the questions. Use your own ideas.**

1. What can you do to protect yourself from crime?

   _____

   _____

2. What can you do to protect yourself from viruses and epidemics?

   _____

   _____

3. What can you do to protect yourself from terrorism?

   _____

   _____

14 **What are the biggest problems facing the world today? Read the list of problems on page 7. Add two of your own ideas to the list.**

Now rate the problems from most important (1) to least important (12).

_____ global warming   _____ antibiotic-resistant bacteria

_____ pollution in the oceans   _____ crime

_____ political corruption   _____ epidemics

_____ war   _____ destruction of the rainforests

_____ drug trafficking   _____ your idea: _____

_____ terrorism   _____ your idea: _____

15   **Choose your top three problems from Exercise 14. Write some ideas for solving them.**

LESSON 4

16   **READING WARM-UP** Some types of problems require thinking up new solutions. Suppose you had lost your keys, and the door to your home was locked. Name at least three solutions you could try.

Adventures in Creative Problem-Solving

Picture this: you're traveling in a foreign city and need to exchange some money but can't find a bank. You ask someone for help, but you don't speak the local language. You flip through a phrase book, but you can't find the right word. Maybe you've been in this hopeless situation yourself. Art Lebedev was, and it inspired him to come up with an idea. He designed a useful T-shirt covered with common symbols for things tourists need, like a restroom, a hotel, or a post office. This allows him to simply point to the symbol on his shirt for the thing he is looking for. It's certainly more painless than carrying a phrase book around! Thinking creatively can help you find a lot of helpful solutions to common problems. Here are a few of our favorite examples of thinking outside the box.

For Safer Buses, Just Add Water!

The Longxiang Bus Company in China was getting many complaints about careless drivers from passengers who were sick of being bumped around. The bad driving had gotten out of control, so the company came up with a creative idea. To encourage purposeful driving, they hung up bowls of water next to each driver. If the driver turned or braked too quickly, the bowl would tip over and spill the water. Drivers were required to have a full bowl of water at the end of their shift—and a dry uniform! Some felt that the company went a little overboard, but the idea was successful. Just like that, the complaints, along with the buses, slowed down.

Sidewalk Art? Watch Where You Step

In Auckland, New Zealand, city leaders had another problem. Absent-minded pedestrians on cell phones were walking into roads and causing accidents. Unbelievably, between 2008 and 2102, almost 750 people were hit by cars at a single intersection! So the government decided on a meaningful and inventive way to get people's attention. They commissioned an artist to create 3-D drawings on sidewalks near busy roads. The realistic pictures showed frightening animals, like sharks and snakes, breaking out of the sidewalk and the words "Don't step into danger." With these eye-catching safety reminders, pedestrians became much more careful.

Video Game Chores: Can I Play?

Parents know what a pain in the neck it is to get children to help out around the house. But again, creative thinking can even make boring chores like doing the laundry almost effortless. How? Take ChoreMonster, a mobile app that turns chores into a game. As children complete chores that parents have programmed into the app, they earn rewards from both the game and their parents. For example, by washing the dishes, a child might earn the chance to see a clip from a new movie—before it hits the theaters!

As these examples show, sometimes all you need to solve a problem is a little imagination. After all, think of how far you can get with a powerful idea—in Art Lebedev's case, it took him all the way around the world!

Now answer the questions.

1. What was Art Lebedev's problem?

   _____

2. What was his solution?

   _____

3. What was the Longxiang Bus Company's problem?

   _____

4. What did they do to solve it?

   _____

5. What was the problem in Auckland?

_____

6. What did the government do to solve the problem?

_____

7. What problem do many parents have?

_____

8. What solution is described in the article?

_____

18 Have you ever experienced a problem that required a creative solution? What did you do?

_____

_____

_____

_____

19 Write sentences using the adjectives in parentheses.

1. (restful) _____

2. (restless) _____

3. (helpful) _____

4. (helpless) _____

5. (pitiful) _____

6. (pitiless) _____

GRAMMAR BOOSTER

A Rewrite each sentence. Change the subject infinitive to a subject complement or begin with an impersonal _it_.

1. To be alone is my biggest fear.

_____

2. To keep track of expenses is the most important part of Sandy's job.

_____

3. To become more outgoing is my goal for this year.

_____

4. To protect the building is the security guard's job.

_____

5. To end political corruption is the purpose of this investigation.

_____

B Write sentences. Use an impersonal <u>it</u> and an infinitive, and a phrase with <u>for</u> + a noun or pronoun.

1. It / important / you / know the rules

   <u>It's important for you to know the rules.</u>

2. It / time / our government / improve public sanitation

   _____

3. It / easy / Jana / learn new vocabulary

   _____

4. It / hard / pessimists / have a positive outlook

   _____

5. It / not necessary / you / clean the kitchen

   _____

C Rewrite each statement in indirect speech.

1. Tom said, "Meet me at 6:30."

   _____

2. Kate said, "Call the client this afternoon."

   _____

3. Alice said, "Don't forget to file the report on time."

   _____

4. Alex told me, "Don't wear fancy jewelry out on the street."

   _____

D Correct the errors in the sentences.

1. It's difficult for me talk in front of large crowds.

2. Ellen's goal to finish this project by the end of the week.

3. He got everyone agree with him.

4. It's too early for to eat dinner.

5. It's my cousin's dream for become a pilot.

6. Tony said don't to be late for the meeting.

E List three ideas under each of the topics below.

1. Activities you enjoy

   _____
   _____
   _____

2. Your goals

   _____
   _____
   _____

3. Good memories

   _____
   _____
   _____

4. To-do list for this week

   _____
   _____
   _____

Now use your lists to complete the sentences. Use gerunds or infinitives.
Make sure the items in each series are parallel.

Example: I enjoy *skiing, running, and painting* _____.

1. I enjoy _____.

2. I intend _____.

3. I recall _____.

4. I need _____.

A **PREWRITING: BRAINSTORMING IDEAS** You will write a paragraph describing either optimists or pessimists. Write words and phrases related to each perspective.

Optimists

have a positive outlook

_____

_____

_____

Pessimists

have a negative outlook

_____

_____

_____

Use your ideas to write a topic sentence for each perspective. (Remember: The topic sentence **introduces** the topic and the focus of the paragraph.)

1. Optimists: _____

2. Pessimists: _____

Choose one of your topic sentences. Write three to five supporting sentences. (Remember: The supporting sentences give **details, examples**, and **other facts** related to the topic sentence.)

1. _____

2. _____

3. _____

4. _____

5. _____

B **WRITING** Write your topic sentence and supporting sentences from Exercise A as a paragraph. End with a concluding sentence. (Remember: The concluding sentence **restates** [gives the same information in different words] the topic sentence or **summarizes** the paragraph.)

_____

_____

_____

_____

_____

_____

_____

_____

C **SELF-CHECK**

☐ Does my paragraph have a topic sentence?

☐ Do the supporting sentences in my paragraph all relate to the topic?

☐ Do I have a concluding sentence?

2 Music and Other Arts

1 Complete the chart.

1. a play or ballet you'd like to see	
2. a movie you'd like to see	
3. a movie you think isn't anything to write home about	
4. your favorite musician or musical group	
5. a musician or group whose music you really don't like	
6. an artist whose work you love	
7. an artist whose work isn't really your thing	
8. a museum that you enjoy visiting or would like to visit	

2 **WHAT ABOUT YOU?** Answer the questions.

1. What was the last music you downloaded? _____

2. Which musician or musical group do you download most often? _____

3. Which of that artist's songs do you like the most? The least? _____

_____

4. Write three sentences about the music you download. Use some of the words from the box.

a beat	a performance	a voice
a melody	a sound	lyrics

_____

_____

_____

3 Read the weekly guide to cultural events. Then write a reaction to each event. Which events would you like to attend and which would you rather not go to? Explain your reasons.

1. Saxon Hall
Q29 in concert: This innovative rock band from Canada always gives a memorable performance. Their sound is a mix of old-time rock and new, danceable beats. Bring your earplugs though—their concerts are known to be loud.

2. Brookstone Theater
Zest for Life, a new play by Theodore Watkins: In this dark comedy, a group of friends reunites ten years after graduating from college. A series of mishaps leads to some hilarious misadventures.

3. City Center
Our own City Ballet troupe performs *Coppélia*: Principal ballerina Sophie Arther dances the title role, in this lovely interpretation of a classic. Also notable are the set's whimsical paintings that form the perfect backdrop for the dance.

4. Cooper Gallery
Theresa Martin, Recent Paintings: If you are a fan of modern art, this show is right up your alley. Martin's large, bold canvases feature bright, intense colors against dark, moody backgrounds.

4 **Read the online review of an event.**

ureviewthearts.com

UREVIEW THE ARTS

1. Event:

Hamilton

2. Type of event:
- ⦿ a musical
- ○ a talk
- ○ a comedy show
- ○ an art exhibit
- ○ a play
- ○ a jazz performance
- ○ a movie
- ○ a rock concert
- ○ a ballet

3. How would you rate this event:
5 stars = best
1 star = worst

- ⦿ ★ ★ ★ ★ ★
- ○ ★ ★ ★ ★
- ○ ★ ★ ★
- ○ ★ ★
- ○ ★

4. Your opinion of the event:

Hamilton is the best thing I've seen in years! Normally, musicals aren't my thing, but this performance blew me away. The lyrics were so intelligent, and the unique hip-hop sound made history really interesting. In addition, the actors' voices were top notch. I highly recommend seeing this musical. *IF* you can get tickets, that is.

Now complete a review of an event you've attended or one you can imagine attending.

ureviewthearts.com

UREVIEW THE ARTS

1. Event:

2. Type of event:
- ○ a musical
- ○ a talk
- ○ a comedy show
- ○ an art exhibit
- ○ a play
- ○ a jazz performance
- ○ a movie
- ○ a rock concert
- ○ a ballet

3. How would you rate this event:
5 stars = best
1 star = worst

- ○ ★ ★ ★ ★ ★
- ○ ★ ★ ★ ★
- ○ ★ ★ ★
- ○ ★ ★
- ○ ★

4. Your opinion of the event:

_____

_____

_____

_____

_____

_____

_____

5 Write a sentence about a song, a band, a performance, or a person you know, using each phrase.

1. nothing to write home about _____

2. isn't my thing _____

3. hard to please _____

4. right up my alley _____

5. a song with fantastic lyrics _____

LESSON 1

6 Complete the questions, using the present perfect continuous or the present perfect. Then answer the questions and provide details.

1. What _____ you _____ to lately? _____
   (listen)

2. _____ you _____ any good movies recently? _____
   (see)

3. _____ you ever _____ in a band or musical group?
   (be)

   _____

4. What types of events _____ you _____ these days?
   (go to)

   _____

5. How long _____ you _____ to your favorite musician?
   (listen)

   _____

7 Check the sentences that are grammatically correct. Rewrite the incorrect sentences, using a correct form of the verb.

1. ☐ I've already been seeing that movie.

   _____

2. ☐ Have you been playing any music lately?

   _____

3. ☐ He's been going to concerts for a while.

   _____

4. ☐ She's been going to three plays this month.

   _____

5. ☐ I've seen Vanessa-Mae in concert twice.

   _____

6. ☐ How many times have you been listening to that song?

   _____

7. ☐ Have you been going to the art museum yet?

   _____

8 Write at least five sentences about singers, bands, or music you don't like. Use the words from the box.

commercial	dated	repetitive	sentimental	serious

Justin Bieber's music is too sentimental for my taste.

_____

_____

_____

_____

9 Complete the conversation about musical tastes. Use your own words. Try to use at least one cleft sentence with **What**.

A: Are you as much of a _____ fan as I am?

B: _____? To be honest, _____.

A: Really? Why?

B: Well, _____.

A: So who *do* you like?

B: Me? I really like _____.

A: You do? _____.

10 Rewrite each statement as a cleft sentence with **What**.

1. Classical music helps me unwind.

   What helps me unwind is classical music.

2. The lyrics in that musical really impressed me.

   _____

3. We really enjoy the music reviews on this radio station.

   _____

4. I miss playing the violin.

   _____

5. I find jazz hard to listen to.

   _____

6. Taylor Swift's music leaves me cold.

   _____

7. I'd like more than anything to see Maná in concert.

   _____

8. We'd really like to hear some live music tonight.

   _____

11 Read about Jeff Thayer's taste in music. Underline the five cleft sentences with <u>What</u>.

I'm not sure when I started really listening to music. I think I was about 14. What I remember best is listening to pop music while I did my homework. Now pop music gets on my nerves. What I prefer now is urban dance music, though I like to listen to jazz or classical when I'm working or studying. My sister is really into music, too but we have different tastes. What she loves is rock music from the 1950s, but that just sounds too dated for me! My taste in music has changed over the years, but what hasn't changed is the role of music in my life. I use it to help me focus and get things done. But what I really like is just to sit back when I have nothing else to do and listen. I've been listening to music for almost ten years now, and I can't imagine what I would do without it. I believe that life would be dull and empty without music.

Jeff Thayer
Detroit, Michigan, USA

Now write a short paragraph about your musical tastes. Try to use cleft sentences with <u>What</u>.
- What types of music do you listen to?
- What do you like about that music?
- Is there anything about that music that you don't like? What is it?
- How have your tastes changed?

LESSON 3

12 **READING WARM-UP** Do you know someone who's gifted? What does this person do well? Describe his or her personality. What are some of this person's positive qualities? Negative qualities?

_____

_____

_____

13 **READING** Have you ever heard of Ray Charles? What do you know about him?

_____

_____

Now read the bibliography.

"I was born with music inside me."

They called him "The Genius"—"the only genius in the [music] business," according to singer Frank Sinatra. What made him a genius is the original way in which he combined the diverse genres of jazz, rhythm and blues, gospel, and country. He broke down the walls that had always existed between musical genres, creating groundbreaking music that has had a huge influence on the course of rock and pop. It has been said that his music can "break your heart or make you dance." His name was Ray Charles, and he was known as "the father of soul."

Ray Charles was born in 1930, into a poor family in the southeastern United States. At age five, he gradually began to lose his vision and was totally blind by age seven.

Charles had shown an interest in music since the age of three. At seven, he left home to attend the Florida School for the Deaf and Blind. There he learned to read, write, and arrange music in Braille and play the piano, organ, saxophone, clarinet, and trumpet. While he was at the school, his mother died. At fifteen, he left school and began working as a traveling jazz musician in Florida, and later in Washington state.

In 1950, Charles moved to Los Angeles, where he found his own unique sound. He combined jazz and blues with gospel music to create his first big hit recording, "I Got a Woman." On "I Got a Woman," Charles began to sing in a more emotional, intense, and exciting voice. He later said, "When I started to sing like myself . . . when I started singing like Ray Charles, it had this spiritual and churchy, this religious or gospel sound." This recording made him famous and marked the beginning of a new musical genre, "soul."

Although Charles had discovered his sound and success, he didn't stop trying new things. Always energetic, he explored new genres and brought his unique style to new audiences. In the 1960s, he had both country and pop hits, with songs like "Georgia on My Mind" and "Hit the Road, Jack."

Throughout his life, Charles continued to write and perform. He also made television and movie appearances. His participation in the 1985 release of "We Are the World" brought a renewed interest in his work.

To this day, Ray Charles remains one of the most important influences on popular music. His passionate singing and intelligent combining of different musical genres is the ideal that many musicians continue to measure their work by.

Ray Charles died on June 10, 2004, at the age of 73. A notorious ladies' man, he is survived by 12 children, 18 grandchildren, and one great-grandchild. In response to the news of his death, singer Aretha Franklin said, "He was a fabulous man, full of humor and wit . . ." Ray Charles possessed all of the positive qualities of a creative personality—he was gifted, energetic, imaginative, and passionate—without displaying the negative qualities that often accompany creative genius. He was not difficult or egotistical. In fact, he was quite humble. In 1983 he said, "Music's been around a long time, and there's going to be music long after Ray Charles is dead. I just want to make my mark, leave something musically good behind."

List at least six adjectives from the reading that describe Ray Charles's music.

_____   _____

_____   _____

_____   _____

Now list five adjectives from the reading that describe Ray Charles's personality.

_____   _____

_____   _____

_____

14 Match the words and phrases from the reading with their definitions. Write the letter on the line.

1. _____ groundbreaking

2. _____ blind

3. _____ Braille

4. _____ gospel

5. _____ soul

6. _____ ladies' man

7. _____ humble

a. a type of music with jazz, blues, and gospel influences that often expresses deep emotions

b. a form of raised printing that blind people can read by touching

c. original and important; showing a new way of doing or thinking about things

d. not considering yourself better than others

e. not able to see

f. a man who enjoys and attracts the company of women

g. a style of religious music associated with the southern U.S.

15 Write a short description of Ray Charles's music, based on the reading.

_____

_____

_____

16 CHALLENGE What do Ludwig van Beethoven and Ray Charles have in common? How are they different? List similarities where the circles overlap and differences in the areas that do not overlap.

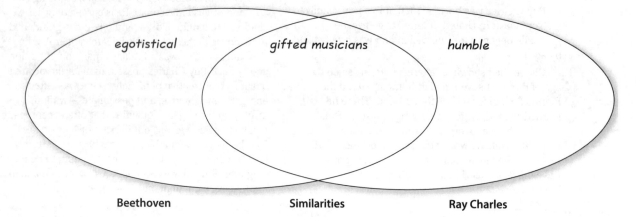

egotistical   gifted musicians   humble

Beethoven   **Similarities**   **Ray Charles**

LESSON 4

17 Complete the sentences with the correct participial adjectives. Use the present or past participle of the underlined verb.

1. Classical music <u>soothes</u> her infant son.

   a. Classical music is _____ to her infant son.

   b. Her infant son is _____ by classical music.

2. Modern art <u>interests</u> Robert.

   a. Robert thinks modern art is _____.

   b. Robert is _____ in modern art.

3. Her piano playing <u>amazes</u> me.

    a. I'm ——————————— by her piano playing.

    b. Her piano playing is ———————————.

4. The movie's sentimental story <u>touched</u> Samantha.

    a. Samantha was ——————————— by the movie.

    b. Samantha found the movie to be very ———————————.

5. Ballet performances <u>bore</u> Eric; he prefers modern dance.

    a. Eric is ——————————— by ballet and prefers to watch modern dance.

    b. Eric thinks ballet is ———————————.

6. Concerts <u>excite</u> Alex and Sophie. They're going to one this Saturday.

    a. Alex and Sophie think concerts are ———————————.

    b. Alex and Sophie are ——————————— about the concert on Saturday.

18 **Circle the correct adjective and then complete each sentence with your own words.**

1. I'm (soothed / soothing) by ———————————.

2. I find ——————————— to be very (entertained / entertaining).

3. I try to avoid ——————————— because it's so (depressed / depressing).

4. I was (disappointed / disappointing) when I found out that ———————————.

5. For me, ——————————— is really (relaxed / relaxing).

6. I'm (pleased / pleasing) that ———————————.

19 **Read the advertisement. Then answer the questions on page 22.**

1. According to the ad, what are five benefits of *Little Genius* CDs?

_____

_____

_____

_____

_____

2. What's your opinion? Do you think listening to music is beneficial for babies? Explain.

_____

_____

GRAMMAR BOOSTER

A **Choose the correct verb form(s) to complete each sentence. In some sentences, two or more verb forms are correct.**

1. He _____ professionally when he was a teenager.

☐ danced   ☐ has danced   ☐ has been dancing

2. They _____ hip-hop music all day, and it's starting to get on my nerves.

☐ played   ☐ have played   ☐ have been playing

3. By the time I got to the concert, my favorite singer _____.

☐ already performed   ☐ had already performed   ☐ had already been performing

4. He _____ that movie last night.

☐ saw   ☐ has seen   ☐ has been seeing

5. She _____ on the lyrics for her new song for hours, but now she's taking a break for dinner.

☐ worked   ☐ has worked   ☐ has been working

6. The actors _____ all afternoon.

☐ were rehearsing   ☐ rehearsed   ☐ have been rehearsing

B **Find the error in each sentence. Rewrite the sentence, using a correct verb form.**

1. What did you listen to lately?

_____

2. Sarah Cho has been playing that CD for me yesterday.

_____

3. I've been watching that video four times already.

_____

4. I was buying that DVD yesterday.

_____

5. How many concerts have you been going to?

_____

6. The performance already began by the time we arrived.

_____

7. When we got to the ticket window, the movie already sold out.

_____

8. Many people have been going to the theater last year.

_____

C Complete the sentences with your own words. Use appropriate verb forms.

1. When I began this class, I had already _____.

2. Before I traveled to _____, I had never _____.

3. I had never seen _____ until _____.

4. I bought the _____ CD after _____.

5. By the time I got home last night, _____.

D Rewrite each question, using a phrase from the box and a noun clause. Use each phrase once.

Do you know	I don't know	I'd like to find out
I can't imagine	I wonder	We're not sure

Example: (What time does the movie start?) _Do you know what time the movie starts?_ _____

1. (Do they like modern jazz?) _____

2. (Where is the concert hall?) _____

3. (Who sings that song?) _____

4. (Does Peter like ballet?) _____

5. (When is that artist's next show?) _____

6. (What would Jen think of this music?) _____

E Complete each statement in your own way.

Example: Many people believe that _there is life on other planets_ _____.

1. Many people believe that _____.

2. My friend argues that _____.

3. Experts recommend that _____.

4. Some people claim that _____.

5. The newspapers report that _____.

Now give your opinion of each statement, using a noun clause as a noun complement.

Example: [The belief . . .] _The belief that there is life on other planets makes sense to me._ _____

1. [The belief . . .] _____

2. [The argument . . .] _____

3. [The recommendation . . .] _____

4. [The claim . . .] _____

5. [The report . . .] _____

A **PREWRITING: TREE DIAGRAM** Choose a friend or family member to describe. Use the tree diagram below to collect details about this person's appearance, personality, interests, and accomplishments.

NAME OF PERSON: _____

Appearance	Personality	Interests	Accomplishments
_____	_____	_____	_____
_____	_____	_____	_____
_____	_____	_____	_____
_____	_____	_____	_____
_____	_____	_____	_____
_____	_____	_____	_____
_____	_____	_____	_____

B **WRITING** Use information from the diagram to write a detailed description of the person you chose. Decide which categories you want to focus on and organize your paragraph(s) thoughtfully. Be sure to use parallel structure.

_____

_____

_____

_____

_____

_____

_____

_____

_____

_____

C **SELF-CHECK**

☐ Does my paragraph have a topic sentence and supporting sentences?

☐ Do I have a concluding sentence?

☐ Did I use parallel structure?

Money, Finance, and You

1 **Check the statements that reflect good spending habits.**

1. ☐ If something is way over your budget, use your credit card.

2. ☐ Cut back on your spending.

3. ☐ Make sure your income is more than your expenses.

4. ☐ If you're feeling down, go shopping.

5. ☐ Try to save up a little for a rainy day.

6. ☐ Occasionally, treat yourself to something you have your heart set on.

7. ☐ If you don't have enough money for something, save up for it.

8. ☐ If you want it, go ahead and shell out the money for it.

9. ☐ Compare prices online before you buy.

10. ☐ If something breaks, try to have it repaired.

2 **Answer the questions.**

1. Have you ever bought something that turned out to be an impulse item? Do you regret buying it? Explain.

_____

_____

_____

2. What is one item you have bought that has turned out to be very useful? Explain.

_____

_____

_____

3. Are you usually a thrifty shopper or an impulse buyer? Explain.

_____

_____

_____

3 **Answer the questions.**

1. What's a minor indulgence (something small and unnecessary) that you spend money
   on regularly? (For example, a daily cup of coffee or a weekly magazine.) _____

2. How much does this indulgence cost? _____

3. Calculate how many times per year you spend money on it. (For example, a cup of
   coffee each weekday: 5 days x 52 weeks = 260 times per year.) _____

4. Multiply the cost (your answer to question 2) by the number of times (your answer to
   question 3). How much money do you spend in a year on your small indulgence? _____

5. Were you surprised by the results? What else would you like to spend that money on?

   _____

4 **Read the article.**

Avoiding Impulse Purchases

Almost all of us have been in this situation: you see something in a store that you just have to have. You buy it on impulse, but once you get home, you realize it's not something you really need. And worse: it's way over your budget. Well, here are some tips to avoid making that impulse purchase next time:

1. Pay cash. Bring only enough money to buy what you need. If you can't charge an extra purchase, you will be much less likely to spend your cash on things you don't need.

2. Make a list of purchases you regret. Keep this list with you when you shop. Looking at it mght make you think twice about new impulse items.

3. Don't be fooled by gimmicks. Ask yourself if the features you like so much add value to the product or are just for show.

4. Don't be misled by sales. Don't buy things just because they are on sale. It doesn't matter how much something is discounted if it's not something that you really need.

5. Lastly, do allow yourself a fun purchase once in a while. You'll be less likely to buy impulse items if you set aside some money to treat yourself occasionally.

Now answer the questions.

1. According to the article, what is wrong with making impulse purchases?

   _____

2. In your own words, explain how making a list of purchases you regret can help you.

   _____

3. Why do you think allowing yourself a fun purchase occasionally helps control impulse purchasing?

   _____

4. Which tip from the article do you think is the most important? Why?

   _____

5. Do you already use any of the tips from the article? Which ones?

   _____

5 Look at the pictures. Why do the people regret their purchases? Complete each explanation with a reason from the box.

costs so much to maintain	is so hard to operate	takes up so much room
just sits around collecting dust	is so hard to put together	

1. "I bought a guitar last summer. I really intended to learn how to play it, but I haven't picked it up for months now. It _____."

2. "I was so excited to get my new smart watch. But it _____. Who can understand all those choices? Not me! What a pain!"

3. "We bought a beautiful crib for our baby, but it's in pieces all over the floor. Unfortunately, the instructions are in Italian, and it _____."

4. "I ordered a new computer online, but I had no idea the monitor would be so big. It _____ on my desk. I should have bought a laptop."

5. "I wish I hadn't bought this boat. I don't use it very often, and it _____. Between the fuel, the docking fees, and the costs to service and clean it, I'm not sure it's worth it."

6 For each item in Exercise 5, write a sentence about the buyer's remorse. Use <u>wish</u> + the past perfect or <u>should have</u> + a past participle.

1. *He wishes he hadn't bought the guitar.* _____

2. _____

3. _____

4. _____

5. _____

7 After completing the Now You Can on Student's Book page 29, write a short paragraph about the item you discussed in Exercise D, Conversation Activator. Summarize why you regret buying it.

LESSON 2

8 Answer each question about your goals. Then, for each answer, write a sentence about your plan for achieving your goal. Use the future perfect or <u>hope</u>, <u>expect</u>, <u>plan</u>, or <u>intend</u> with perfect infinitives.

Example: What's something expensive that you hope to buy? *a laptop computer*

    I will have saved enough to buy a laptop by next March.

1. What's something expensive that you hope to buy? _____

_____

2. Do you have a debt you'd like to pay off? What is it? _____

_____

3. What is one way you can cut back on your spending and save more each month? _____

_____

4. What is one of your career goals? _____

_____

5. Your education significantly affects your ability to make money. What is one of your education goals?

_____

_____

6. Fitness can involve playing sports, exercising, or eating healthily. What fitness goal do you have?

_____

_____

9 What will you have done by the year 2025? Write a short paragraph. Use the future perfect or <u>hope</u>, <u>expect</u>, <u>intend</u>, or <u>plan</u> and a perfect infinitive.

Example: <u>By the year 2025, I will have finished law school. I expect to have bought a house</u>
<u>by then. I hope to have gotten married and started a family.</u>

LESSON **3**

10 Read the conversation. Try to determine the meaning of the underlined phrases from their context.

> **A:** What's wrong? You look a little worried.
>
> **B:** Oh, just worried about money.
>
> **A:** Why? You <u>make a good living</u>.
>
> **B:** You're right, I do. But I still seem to live paycheck to paycheck.
>
> **A:** Well, have you made yourself a budget?
>
> **B:** Sort of . . . But I don't <u>stick to it</u>.
>
> **A:** And what about credit card bills? Do you pay them on time? And do you pay them in full?
>
> **B:** I pay them on time, but I usually just <u>pay the minimum</u>. So the next month my bill is even higher, and I <u>never catch up</u>.
>
> **A:** Well, I bet you know this, but don't <u>charge</u> anything you can't pay for at the end of the month. And see if you can cut back enough to pay off those bills a little bit each month. I bet in a few months you'll have <u>made a dent in your debt</u>.
>
> **B:** Those are good suggestions. Thanks. I guess I do need to work on <u>managing my money</u> well.

Now match the words and phrases with their definitions. Write the letter on the line.

1. _____ pay the minimum   **a.** practice good spending and saving habits

2. _____ never catch up   **b.** pay the least amount required

3. _____ stick to a budget   **c.** pay a partial amount, but enough to be noticeable

4. _____ charge   **d.** pay with a credit card

5. _____ make a dent in a debt   **e.** earn enough money to be comfortable

6. _____ manage your money   **f.** only spend the money you've planned to spend

7. _____ make a good living   **g.** can't get out of debt

11 **Choose the best choice to complete each statement.**

1. Big spenders are more likely to _____.
   a. be drowning in debt
   b. be frugal
   c. stick to a budget

2. Cheapskates generally _____.
   a. use credit cards often
   b. have a lot of stuff
   c. keep track of their expenses

3. Big spenders are usually _____.
   a. generous
   b. stingy
   c. frugal

4. Thrifty people are more likely to _____.
   a. be wiped out by a job loss
   b. stick to a budget
   c. let their bills get out of hand

5. Thrifty people generally _____.
   a. live beyond their means
   b. are drowning in debt
   c. pay their credit cards in full

> The world record for owning the most credit cards is held by Walter Cavanagh of Santa Clara, California, US. He has 1,497 cards, which together are worth more than $1.7 million in credit.

12 **Read the article.**

Financial Planning
Five Benefits of Keeping a Budget

1. A budget allows you to spend money on things you really need or want. A budget requires you to keep track of your expenses. You see where your money actually goes and plan where to cut back on spending. The money you used to spend daily on little things like coffee or taxis can go toward something more important.

2. A budget can keep you out of debt. With a budget, you know whether or not you're living within your means. If you use credit cards, this may not be obvious. You might have extra cash at the end of each month and think that you're OK. But, if you're not paying your credit card bills in full, you're probably living beyond your means.

3. A budget can make you better prepared for emergencies. A budget requires you to put some money away in savings. So, if you find yourself in a difficult situation or faced with unexpected expenses, you'll have some extra money you can fall back on.

4. A budget can help you reach your savings goals. Whatever you are saving for, you need a plan that tells you how much you have, how much you need to spend, and how much you can save.

5. A budget gives you peace of mind because it allows you to stop worrying about how you're going to make ends meet.

Now answer the questions.

1. According to the article, why is it important to keep track of your expenses?

   _____

2. According to the article, why can using credit cards be a problem?

   _____

3. Why can a budget make you better prepared for emergencies?

   _____

4. Which benefit from the article do you think is the most important? Why?

   _____

13 **READING WARM-UP** Complete the chart with information about a charity you are familiar with.

Name of charity	Who they help	What they do
CARE	poor people all over the world	work to reduce poverty and solve problems in poor communities—through education, health care, etc.

Have you ever donated money to a charity? What was the name of the organization or cause? Why did you make a donation?

_____

_____

_____

14 **READING** Read the article on three charities.

World Wildlife Fund

The World Wildlife Fund (WWF) is known worldwide by its panda logo. WWF has been working for almost 50 years in more than 100 countries around the globe to conserve nature and the diversity of life on Earth. With more than 5 million members worldwide, WWF is the world's largest privately-financed conservation organization. It leads international efforts to protect animals, plants, and natural areas. Its global goals are:

1. to save endangered species—especially giant pandas, tigers, threatened whales and dolphins, rhinos, elephants, marine turtles, and great apes.
2. to protect the habitats where these endangered species and other wild animals live.
3. to address threats to the natural environment—such as pollution, over-fishing, and climate change.

The International Rescue Committee

Working in 40 countries, the International Rescue Committee (IRC) has been responding to crises around the globe for over 80 years. Their goal is to: "help to restore health, safety, education, economic

(continued on page 32)

(continued)

wellbeing, and power to people devastated by conflict and disaster." In 2015, the IRC and its partner organizations helped 23 million people around the world. IRC's priorities include:

1. emergency relief: IRC teams arrive on the scene of an emergency or disaster within 72 hours, with doctors and other workers bringing healthcare, food, clean water, and other emergency assistance.
2. lasting solutions: One of the IRC's guiding principles is to help people make their communities stronger and more stable, so that the people they help will be self-sufficient after IRC teams leave. To this end, IRC teams remain on location as long as necessary to help people recover and rebuild.
3. refugee assistance and resettlement: Another key component of the IRC's work is the resettlement of refugees in the U.S. With 26 offices across the U.S., a network of IRC staff and volunteers provides services such as housing, job placement, English-language classes, and medical care to newly-arrived refugees.

The United Nations Children's Fund

The United Nations Children's Fund (UNICEF) is active in 157 countries and territories around the world. The organization works to improve the lives of children worldwide. Its mission is to ensure every child's right to health, education, equality, and protection. UNICEF's priorities are:

1. ensuring quality basic education for all children, especially girls.
2. reaching every child with vaccines and other life-saving health services.
3. building protective environments to keep children safe from violence, abuse, and exploitation.
4. preventing the spread of HIV/AIDS among young people and from parent to child and providing care for those already affected.
5. giving each and every child the best start in life—through health services, good nutrition, safe water, and early learning activities.

Now complete the chart with information from the reading.

Name of charity	Who they help	What they do

15 To which of the three charities in Exercise 14 would you consider making a contribution? Is there one you wouldn't want to give money to? What are your reasons for donating or not donating?

_____

_____

_____

GRAMMAR BOOSTER

A Rewrite the past unreal conditional sentences, using the inverted form.

1. I would have bought a smaller exercise machine if I had realized it would take up so much room.
   Had I realized it would take up so much room, I would have bought a smaller exercise machine.

2. I wouldn't have bought such an expensive car if I had known it would cost so much to maintain.
   _____

3. If I had known these bookshelves would be so hard to put together, I would have asked a friend to help me.
   _____

4. If I had realized the music at last night's concert would be so commercial, I might not have bought tickets.
   _____

5. I might have purchased a different DVR if the salesperson had told me it would be so hard to operate.
   _____

6. Would you have stayed at your job if your boss hadn't been such a tyrant?
   _____

7. If I had known this bread-making machine would just sit around collecting dust, I would have given it to my sister.
   _____

8. If my apartment building had allowed pets, I would have stayed there.
   _____

B What are your plans? For each item, write a sentence about what you will be doing. Use the future continuous.

1. Next Monday, I _____.
2. This weekend I _____.
3. Next year I _____.
4. Five years from now, I _____.
5. At this time next week, _____.
6. When _____, I _____.
7. I _____ while _____.

C Look at the schedules of two sisters. Write sentences comparing the activities of Teresa and Tina Lee for each day. Use a time clause with <u>while</u> and the future continuous.

Teresa Lee

Thursday	work
Friday	work
Saturday	clean the house
Sunday	do laundry

Tina Lee

Thursday	pack for weekend trip with friends
Friday	lie on the beach
Saturday	go horseback riding
Sunday	play tennis

1. Thursday: _While Teresa Lee is working, Tina Lee is going to be packing for a trip._
2. Friday: _____
3. Saturday: _____
4. Sunday: _____

D Complete the chart with three of your hobbies or activities and the year in which you started each.

Hobby / activity	When started

Now use the information in the chart to complete the sentences, using the future perfect continuous.

Example: By the year 2018, _I will have been collecting stamps for 20 years_.

1. By the year 2020, _____.
2. By next year, _____.
3. By the time I _____, I _____.

A **PREWRITING: LISTING IDEAS** Choose an idea for a new local charity. Think of a name and goal for your charity. Write them on the notepad and list several ways your charity will benefit the community.

Some ideas

- An organization to improve city parks
- An after-school program for young children
- A fund to provide housing for the homeless
- An organization to help stray animals
- A soup kitchen
- Your own idea: _____

WRITING MODEL

The mission of People for City Park is to clean up the park and improve the green space, playground, and community stage. There are many ways this charity will benefit the community. Most importantly, it will make the park a clean, safe, and fun place for families to spend time outdoors. Right now, people don't spend time in the park, because it is dirty, with outdated playground equipment. We will change that. Secondly, once the community stage is fixed up, we will once more be able to host concerts and other cultural events in our park. And, last but not least, just having a place to walk or sit and look at the flowers will make everyone in the neighborhood feel better.

Name of charity:

Goal:

How it will benefit community:

B **WRITING** Write a paragraph, using ideas from your notepad. Your topic sentence should state your charity's goal. Include at least three potential benefits of your charity. Organize your ideas in order of importance.

_____

_____

_____

_____

_____

_____

C **SELF-CHECK**

☐ Did I present my ideas in order of importance?

☐ Did I use words and phrases to indicate their relative importance?

☐ Did I use correct punctuation?

Clothing and Appearance

1 **Look at the hairstyles. Then answer the questions.**

bob   afro   man bun   mohawk

quiff   mullet   shag   bouffant

1. Do you find any of these hairstyles attractive? Which ones? _____

   _____

2. Do you find any of these hairstyles unattractive? Which ones? _____

   _____

3. Do any of the hairstyles look modern, like you might see them in a fashion magazine today? _____

   _____

4. Which hairstyles are attention-getting? _____

   _____

5. Which hairstyles look like they take a lot of time to maintain? _____

   _____

6. Would you consider any of these hairstyles for yourself? Which one(s)? _____

   _____

2 Describe clothing that you own or have seen in stores or online for each category.

1. something trendy: _____
2. something classic: _____
3. something funky: _____
4. something fashionable: _____
5. something elegant: _____
6. something loud: _____
7. something subdued: _____
8. something frumpy: _____
9. something that attracts too much attention: _____
10. something you wouldn't be caught dead in: _____

LESSON 1

3 Write sentences to describe the clothing in the photos. Use as much vocabulary as you can.

① ② ③ ④ ⑤ ⑥

1. _He's wearing a pretty stylish outfit: a dress shirt, a plaid blazer, and solid-color pants._

2. _____

3. _____

4. _____

5. _____

6. _____

4 Write sentences to describe what you would wear to each event.

1. an office party _____

2. the ballet _____

3. a rock concert _____

4. a formal wedding _____

5. an important meeting _____

6. a comedy show _____

5 **CHALLENGE** Read the quote from 1930s fashion designer Elsa Schiaparelli. Then answer the questions.

> "Ninety percent [of women] are afraid of being conspicuous and of what people will say. So they buy a gray suit. They should dare to be different."

1. Rewrite Ms. Schiaparelli's fashion advice in your own words.

_____

_____

2. Do you think this is good fashion advice for people (not just women) today? Why or why not?

_____

_____

In the summer of 2005, both the Japanese and Chinese governments asked office workers to dress down to save energy. A majority of Japanese companies complied with the "Cool Biz" no-tie, no-jacket campaign to reduce air-conditioner use. In Japan, about 210 million kilowatt hours of electricity were saved, reducing carbon dioxide emissions by about 79,000 tons.

LESSON 2

6 Read the opinions of casual business dress. Check the statements you agree with.

1. ☐ What's important is to act like a professional. If you're confident and good at your job, you can be just as effective in jeans and a nice shirt as in a suit and tie.

2. ☐ I think casual dress is appropriate for most offices, as long as one's appearance is clean and neat.

3. ☐ I believe that when people dress like professionals, they act more professionally.

4. ☐ I think dress-down day is a pain in the neck. I never know what to wear. What does "business casual" really mean?

5. ☐ People have taken casual dress codes too far! A number of companies have actually had to introduce "business formal days."

6. ☐ I don't think casual dress creates a good image for a company, especially if the company does business internationally.

7. ☐ Casually dressed employees are better workers because people are more productive when they're comfortable.

7 Now summarize the opinions in Exercise 6. Complete each statement below with a quantifier from the box.

a couple of	a number of	four	most	some
a few	each	half of	one	three
a majority of	every	many	several	two

1. _____ person expressed an opinion about business casual dress.

2. _____ people think business casual is a good idea.

3. _____ people think business casual is a bad idea.

4. _____ people think that dress and behavior are related.

5. _____ person thinks business casual is annoying.

8 Now rewrite statements 1–4 from Exercise 7, using different quantifiers with similar meanings.

1. _____

2. _____

3. _____

4. _____

CHALLENGE Judging from the statements in Exercise 6, do you think casual business dress is

on the way out? Why or why not? _____

LESSON 3

9 **READING** Read the article.

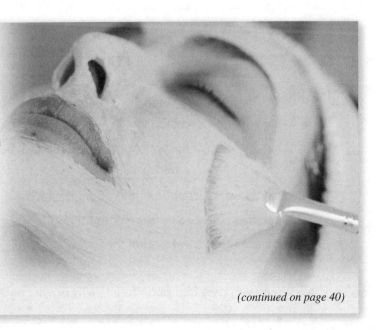

Bird-poop Facials

In some cultures, it is considered good luck to have a bird's droppings land on you. But would you pay to have bird excrement rubbed onto your skin? That's just what some people in cities around the world have begun doing.

"Bird-poop facials" have been around since the 1600s, but they have only recently become popular. The droppings are collected from one type of bird, the Japanese Bush Warbler. They are then disinfected, dried, powdered, and mixed with rice bran. The facial is often referred

(continued on page 40)

Bird-poop Facials *(continued)*

to as being made from nightingale droppings, but the Japanese Bush Warbler is not really a nightingale.

If you cringe at the thought of having bird waste on your face, you are not alone. "Most people who come to us for the first time are a little worried about the smell," says Naomi Rogers, who owns a spa in New York where the facials are performed. "But the majority of them say that it just smells like rice, and they leave looking and feeling wonderful." Many people who swear by bird-poop facials, including several celebrities, say that benefits include healing skin problems such as acne, exfoliating dead skin cells, brightening and softening the skin, and lightening age spots. After a recent facial, Christa Sims reported, "My friends told me I looked five years younger."

But does science back up the claims made by proponents of the facials? Only to a certain point. Guanine, an amino acid found in the bird-poop, does lighten dark skin spots. And urea, also found in the bird waste, may help skin retain moisture. But the improvements in skin tone and texture can probably be achieved just as easily with an exfoliating scrub or mask from the drugstore, says Dr. Anna Fitzgibbon, a dermatologist in Los Angeles.

The facials do come with a steep price tag—almost US $200 in some cities. It is also possible to purchase the ingredients for at-home, do-it-yourself treatments, and these are much less expensive. However, if you do decide to try a bird-poop facial at home, be sure to purchase supplies from a reputable seller, as some products are not actually from the Japanese Bush Warbler or are mixed with other ingredients.

Now complete the statements with words from the box.

facial	proponent	steep price tag
nightingale	reputable	swear by

1. A _____ is a type of bird.

2. A _____ is a treatment that improves the skin of the face.

3. A _____ business is one that you can trust.

4. If you _____ something, you think it's very effective.

5. If something has a _____, it is very expensive.

6. A _____ of something is a supporter of it.

10 **Answer the questions about the article.**

1. What are bird-poop facials? _____

2. What are some of the benefits of bird-poop facials, according to some people? _____

_____

3. What does Dr. Fitzgibbon think about the facials? _____

4. What does Christa Sims think about them? _____

5. What are some drawbacks of the facials? _____

_____

6. Would you try a bird-poop facial? Why or why not? _____

_____

11 Complete the sentences with your own ideas.

1. People who are self-confident generally _____.

2. If you have low self-esteem, you might have trouble _____.

3. If you have high self-esteem, _____.

4. People who are self-centered tend to _____.

5. People who are self-critical might _____.

12 Answer the questions.

1. Do you think that most people are happy with their appearance, or that a majority would like to change their appearance? _____

2. What would you consider doing to change your appearance? _____
_____

3. How far is too far? Which ways of changing one's appearance do you think are inappropriate, tacky, or shocking? _____
_____
_____

13 Look at the ad. Then answer the questions.

1. How would you describe the man in this ad?

_____
_____
_____
_____

IN AS LITTLE AS 2 WEEKS

BUY NOW!!!
Limited time offer.
No more sit ups!
CALL NOW!

2. Do you think that the man in this ad reflects how most men look? Explain.

_____
_____

3. Do you think men are more or less self-conscious than women are about their appearance? Explain.

_____
_____

A Read each statement. Check the meaning of the quantifier in each sentence.

	Some	Not many / Not much
1. Few people were dressed appropriately for the event.	☐	☐
2. There are a few really good books on fashion here.	☐	☐
3. I've got a little money put away for a rainy day.	☐	☐
4. I have little interest in pop music.	☐	☐
5. There are few hairstyles that look good on me.	☐	☐
6. There's a little cake left, if you'd like a piece.	☐	☐

B Add <u>of</u> to the sentences that need it.

1. Several*of* his co-workers wear suits to work.

2. A few friends are coming over for dinner on Friday night.

3. A few my friends are going to a movie tonight.

4. Both dresses look great on you.

5. A majority people still dress up to go to the theater.

6. This is the most traffic I've ever seen on this road.

7. Each the employees voted on whether or not to dress down on Fridays.

8. Some my friends care about fashion, but most do not.

C Complete each sentence with a phrase from the box. Change the verb as necessary to agree with the subject.

be quite good	dress casually	wear contact lenses
be self-confident	have tattoos	be self-centered

1. Most of my friends _____.

2. A lot of pop music _____.

3. Several of my classmates _____.

4. One of my family members _____.

5. None of the people I know _____.

6. A number of celebrities _____.

A **PREWRITING: Y-CHART** Choose one of the topics from the box.

> - Compare and contrast what you and someone you know well do to make yourselves more attractive.
> - Compare and contrast what people today do to make themselves more attractive with what they did twenty years ago.
> - Compare and contrast what celebrities do to make themselves more attractive with what average people do.

Complete the diagram below. Fill in the boxes with the two topics being compared. List differences for each topic first. Then fill in the similarities.

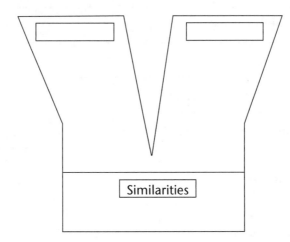

Similarities

B **WRITING** Write two paragraphs to compare and contrast the people for the topic you chose.
- In your first paragraph, write about the similarities. Remember to use connecting words such as <u>like</u>, <u>similarly</u>, <u>likewise</u>, <u>as well</u>, and <u>not either</u>.
- In your second paragraph, write about the differences. Remember to use connecting words such as <u>unlike</u>, <u>in contrast</u>, <u>however</u>, and <u>while</u> / <u>whereas</u>.

_____

_____

_____

_____

_____

_____

_____

_____

_____

C **SELF-CHECK**
- ☐ Did I use connecting words for comparing?
- ☐ Did I use connecting words for contrasting?
- ☐ Does each paragraph have a topic sentence?

Communities

1 Think about a place you have lived in or visited. Then complete the chart with your opinions.

Name of place: _____	
Type of location	
Things you like about the place	
Things you dislike about the place	
Trends (general changes taking place) there	
Things that could be done to improve life there	

2 Read the e-mail message.

● ● ●

From: Jessica@summitmail.com
To: Loretta@summitmail.com
Subject: City Girl

Hey! How's life treating you? I'm busy applying to universities. Can you believe I'm graduating from secondary school this year? I'm thinking about going to a university in an urban area. I know I've always been a country girl, but I think a faster pace might be a nice change. Any advice? Let me know what you think.

Now respond to the e-mail message. Do you think a move to the city is a good idea? Explain your opinion. Describe some advantages and disadvantages of life in the city. If you can, give advice on living in a city.

● ● ●

From: Loretta@summitmail.com
To: Jessica@summitmail.com
Subject: City Girl

_____
_____
_____
_____
_____

3 Write a sentence using each expression in parentheses.

1. (take some getting used to) <u>Living in a high-rise apartment building takes some getting used to.</u>

2. (mind their own business) _____

3. (a mixed blessing) _____

4. (look on the bright side) _____

5. (look out for each other) _____

6. (mean well) _____

7. (has a lot to offer) _____

LESSON 1

4 Judge the appropriateness of each behavior below. Write sentences, using adjectives from Student's Book page 52 or your own adjectives.

1. Using a hand-held phone while driving: <u>It's unsafe to use a hand-held phone while driving.</u>

2. Taking a call in a movie theater: _____

3. Turning your cell phone off in class: _____

4. Having a loud, personal conversation on the train: _____
_____

5. Talking on the phone while shopping: _____

6. Turning your phone to silent mode in a restaurant: _____
_____

7. Leaving your phone on during a flight: _____

Cell-phone use at public cultural events—such as plays, movies, concerts, and art exhibits—is now against the law in New York City. The penalty for violating the law is a fifty-dollar fine and removal from the theater, museum, etc. The law was passed in 2003 after two famous actors reacted to cell-phone users during Broadway performances. In mid-performance, Kevin Spacey turned to a member of the audience who had answered a cell phone and said, "Tell them you're busy." Laurence Fishburne wasn't as polite. When an audience member answered a phone during one of his performances, he yelled, "Turn your @#?! phone off!"*

*Symbols such as @#?! are used to politely denote curse words.

5 Combine each pair of sentences, using a possessive gerund.

1. He sleeps in class. What do you think about it?

<u>What do you think about his sleeping in class?</u>

2. Julie's husband checks his text messages constantly. She can't stand it.

_____

(continued on page 46)

3. Patricia's co-workers call her Patty. She resents it.

_____

4. They complain all the time. I'm so tired of it.

_____

5. We take calls during dinner. Our father objects to it.

_____

6. I hum while I work. Do you mind?

_____

7. You are late so often. Mr. Yu objects to it.

_____

6 Write a check mark next to the sentences that are correct. Correct the incorrect sentences.

1. ☐ Rachel's texting during the meal was annoying me.

2. ☐ Do you mind Paul playing music at night?

3. ☐ Jane chewing gum during the concert was rude.

4. ☐ Sam talking back to his mother is disrespectful.

5. ☐ We don't mind them arriving late.

6. ☐ Them smoking in the hallway is unacceptable.

7. ☐ Sally's not picking up after her dog is inexcusable.

8. ☐ Does my friend talking loudly bother you?

LESSON 2

7 Offer acceptable alternatives for each inappropriate behavior. Use <u>either</u> . . . <u>or</u>.

1. Littering: _People should either throw their garbage in a trash can or hold on to it until they find one._

2. Talking during a movie: _____

3. Playing loud music on a bus: _____

4. Gossiping: _____

5. Eating in class: _____

8 Rewrite each sentence, using <u>neither</u> . . . <u>nor</u> and the antonym of the adjective.

1. Listening to loud music and getting in and out of your seat constantly are inconsiderate on a flight.

Neither listening to loud music nor getting in and out of your seat constantly is considerate on a flight.

2. Leaving a cell phone on and putting your feet up on the seat in front of you are discourteous in a movie theater.

_____

3. Talking on a cell phone and smoking while driving are irresponsible.

_____

4. Talking or laughing while the teacher is talking is disrespectful.

_____

5. Touching the art and taking flash photography in a museum are inappropriate.

_____

9 **Read the pet peeves of visitors to a website.**

Pet Peeves

💬 **Comment**   ➤ **Share**

Name: Sam
I really can't understand why people slow down to stare at traffic accidents. It creates huge, unnecessary traffic jams, and it's dangerous. A driver who's looking at an accident is not looking at the road in front of him—and could cause another accident!   Like • Reply • 1 hr 58 mins

Name: Karen
What gets to me is people who don't cover their mouths when they cough. It really bugs me when a server in a restaurant coughs, spreading germs all over my food. Waiters and waitresses around the world, please wait until you leave the table to cough. If you can't, at least cover your mouth.   Like • Reply • 1 hr 42 mins

Name: Amy
I can't stand dog owners' taking their dogs for walks and not cleaning up after them. If you won't take responsibility for your dog's messes, then don't have a pet!   Like • Reply • 1 hr 27 mins

Name: Will
It really gets on my nerves when salespeople won't interrupt their personal conversations to help me, a paying customer. Ignoring customers is rude and bad for business.   Like • Reply • 1 hr 23 mins

Name: Isabella
I ride my bike a lot—to school, to work, basically wherever I need to go. The thing that ticks me off is drivers who don't use their turn signals and who don't look behind them before they open their car doors. They create a real danger for us cyclists.   Like • Reply • 1 hr 12 mins

Now rate the pet peeves according to how annoying they are to you. Number them from 1 (most annoying) to 6 (least annoying).

_____ drivers who slow down to stare at traffic accidents

_____ servers who don't cover their mouths when they cough

_____ dog owners who don't clean up after their dogs

_____ salespeople who don't interrupt their personal conversations to help you

_____ drivers who don't use their turn signals

_____ drivers who don't look behind them before they open their car doors

10 **CHALLENGE** Now read the pet peeves in Exercise 9 again. Write a sentence summarizing each person's opinion. Use the paired conjunctions in parentheses.

1. Sam's opinion (not only . . . but also): <u>Not only does slowing down to stare at traffic accidents</u>
<u>create huge, unnecessary traffic jams, but it's also dangerous.</u>

2. Karen's opinion (either . . . or): _____
_____

3. Amy's opinion (either . . . or): _____
_____

4. Will's opinion (not only . . . but): _____
_____

5. Isabella's opinion (neither . . . nor): _____
_____

11 **WHAT ABOUT YOU?** What's your pet peeve? Post a message to the message board. Use the messages in Exercise 9 as a guide.

_____
_____
_____
_____

LESSON 3

12 **READING WARM-UP** Think about a park, garden, or playground in your city or town. Who spends time there? What do people do there? Is it a safe place?

_____
_____
_____
_____
_____

Greener Is Safer

It used to be assumed that urban green spaces, such as parks and gardens, fostered crime by providing space for criminals to gather. However, evidence now appears to suggest that just the opposite is true. With concern mounting over the environment, more and more cities around the world have been focusing on creating green spaces — areas with grass, plants, and trees — within city limits. One possibly unexpected result of these green spaces has been a reduction in crime in the neighborhoods directly adjacent to the green areas.

Studies in several large cities in the U.S. and other countries have shown significant reductions in crime in neighborhoods where vacant lots and abandoned industrial sites have been converted to green areas. A project in Philadelphia, Pennsylvania, turned 4,500 vacant lots into areas where residents could gather and enjoy being outside. One result? Gun crimes in the neighborhoods around the green areas decreased significantly. Similarly, a study in Chicago, Illinois, found that low-income housing that was surrounded by trees and other plants had an approximately 50% lower crime rate than the same type of housing without greenery.

What accounts for these improvements? Researchers aren't sure, but there are several factors at work. First, green areas give community residents a space to gather outside, where they not only enjoy their surroundings, but also meet and get to know each other, forming social ties. Neighbors who have formed these ties are more likely to look out for each other. When criminals see a neighborhood with well-cared-for public areas, they know that residents who live there are more likely to support and protect one another, and, therefore, they tend to stay away.

Second, studies have shown that spending time in nature, or even just being exposed to images of the natural world, helps people relax and reduces aggression. Less aggression results in less crime. It may be that simply having contact with green areas makes would-be criminals less likely to commit crimes.

Some cities plan their green spaces while other cities include a combination of professionally-planned spaces along with areas that residents are allowed to plant as they choose. Crime has been shown to be lower in both types of situations. Though lower crime is not by any means the only benefit of urban green spaces, it appears to be yet another reason for cities to include as much greenery as possible as they continue to evolve.

Now answer the questions.

1. What did people used to think about green spaces in cities? _____

   _____

2. How have the beliefs about urban green spaces changed in recent years? _____

   _____

3. Why are more cities including green spaces in their urban planning? _____

   _____

4. What did researchers discover in Philadelphia? _____

   _____

5. According to the article, what are two possible reasons for reduced crime near urban green spaces?

   _____

   _____

6. What is your opinion of the two reasons you listed in item 5? _____

   _____

7. Do you agree that less aggression equals less crime? Explain. _____

   _____

14 Imagine that there is a vacant lot in your neighborhood. How would you design the area as a public green space? Complete the chart.

What would you include?	Why would you include it?

LESSON 4

15 **READING WARM-UP** Check the community service activities that you or someone you know has done.

☐ plant flowers or trees   ☐ collect signatures

☐ pick up trash   ☐ volunteer

☐ mail letters   ☐ make arrangements to donate your organs

☐ make phone calls   ☐ donate money

☐ raise money   ☐ other: _____

Now write sentences.

Example: Write about two activities you or someone you know has done. Use <u>not only</u> . . . <u>but also</u>.
 Not only have I raised money, but I've also volunteered.

1. Write about two activities you or someone you know has done. Use <u>not only</u> . . . <u>but also</u>.

_____

2. Write about two activities you haven't done. Use <u>neither</u> . . . <u>nor</u>.

_____

3. Write about two activities you'd like to do. Use <u>either</u> . . . <u>or</u>.

_____

Volunteer Vacations

Bud Philbrook and Michele Gran were married in 1979. Instead of taking a honeymoon cruise to the Caribbean, they decided to spend a week in a rural village in Guatemala, where they helped raise money for an irrigation system. When they returned to their home in St. Paul, Minnesota, U.S., the local newspaper wrote a story about their unusual honeymoon. Soon, people started contacting them, asking how they could plan a similar trip. Philbrook said, "We knew there was a need in rural communities around the world, and now we were learning people wanted to do this."

In 1984, the couple founded Global Volunteers, a nonprofit agency for people who want to spend their vacation helping others. Now the organization sends about 2,000 people each year to community development programs in seventeen countries on five continents. These short-term volunteer service projects focus on helping children and their families reach their full potential.

Volunteers are invited by local community leaders to work on projects that community members have identified as important. Not only do volunteers work side by side with local people, but they also live in the community. In most cases, no special skills are required. Anyone who wants to be of service and to learn about other cultures can volunteer. Global Volunteers' working vacations are popular with people of all ages. There are young, single volunteers and retired volunteers.

More recently, Global Volunteers has started offering programs for families with children as young as five. Some Global Volunteers community service opportunities include:

- helping to upgrade community buildings in Tanzanian villages.

- caring for infants with special needs in a Romanian hospital.

- tutoring orphaned and abandoned children in India.

- teaching conversational English in Havana or rural Cuba.

Now answer questions about the article.

1. Where did Bud Philbrook and Michele Gran go on their honeymoon? _____

2. What did they do? _____

3. Why do you think they decided to spend their honeymoon in this way?

   _____

4. What effect did their story have on some people who read it?

   _____

5. What did Bud Philbrook and Michele Gran do as a result of people's interest in their trip?

   _____

17 **WHAT ABOUT YOU?** Would you consider a volunteer vacation? Answer the questions.

1. In my opinion, a volunteer vacation would be _____.
   a. a life-changing experience   c. more trouble than it's worth
   b. an adventure   d. kind of scary
   Explain your answer: _____

2. Some Global Volunteers live with local families. How comfortable would you be doing the same
   thing? _____
   a. very comfortable   c. a little uncomfortable
   b. somewhat comfortable   d. very uncomfortable
   Explain your answer: _____

3. At what stage in your life would you want to go on a volunteer vacation? _____
   a. young and single   c. married with a family
   b. married without kids   d. retired
   Explain your answer: _____

4. Which of the community services listed in the article would you want to do? Why?
   _____

5. Would you prefer to volunteer in a rural area or in a city? Why?
   _____

GRAMMAR BOOSTER

A Rewrite each sentence, using the word in parentheses. Make verb changes as necessary.

1. John Coltrane was a great jazz musician, and so was Miles Davis. (too)
   John Coltrane was a great jazz musician, and Miles Davis was, too.

2. The restaurant doesn't allow smoking, and neither does the bar. (not either)
   _____

3. Her company has adopted a casual dress code on Fridays, and his has, too. (so)
   _____

4. Shorts aren't appropriate in the office, and neither are jeans. (not either)
   _____

5. She was annoyed by his behavior, and we were, too. (so)
   _____

6. We've decided to volunteer, and so have they. (too)
   _____

7. Dave Clark doesn't like the city, and we don't either. (neither)
   _____

8. We're not going on vacation this summer, and they're not either. (neither)
   _____

B Complete the diagram to compare two cities that you know. Consider things like traffic, weather, population, natural setting, architecture, infrastructure, and tourist attractions. Write similarities where the circles overlap and differences in the areas that do not overlap.

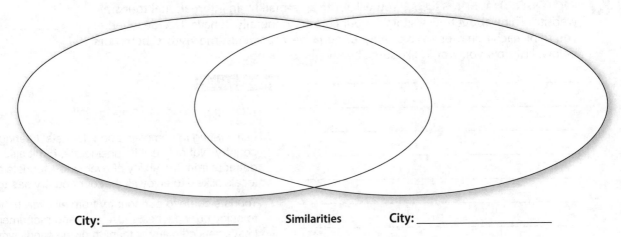

City: _____   Similarities   City: _____

Now use the information from your diagram to write sentences about ways in which the two cities are similar. Use conjunctions with <u>so</u>, <u>too</u>, <u>neither</u>, and <u>not either</u>.

1. _____

2. _____

3. _____

4. _____

5. _____

C Use short responses with <u>so</u>, <u>too</u>, <u>neither</u>, or <u>not either</u> to agree with the statements.

1. **A:** I don't really like the fast pace of life in the city.

   B: _____

2. **A:** I'm really annoyed by smoking in restaurants.

   B: _____

3. **A:** I try to be courteous about using my cell phone.

   B: _____

4. **A:** I can't understand why people talk during movies.

   B: _____

5. **A:** I speak up when something bothers me.

   B: _____

6. **A:** I don't have time to get involved with my community.

   B: _____

7. **A:** I would consider donating my organs.

   B: _____

A **PREWRITING: LISTING IDEAS** You will write an e-mail to an international tourism website. Think about how visitors to your country generally behave. Decide whether you think each behavior has a positive or negative impact. List the visitors' behaviors below. List how you would like some behaviors to change.

_____

_____

_____

_____

_____

_____

_____

_____

_____

_____

WRITING MODEL

http://globalcourtesy.com/soundoff

I am writing to complain about tourists' littering in our country. Not only is it inconsiderate, but it also detracts from the ability of everyone—tourists and locals alike—to enjoy all that our country has to offer.

Tourists come to our country from all over the world to enjoy our beaches, museums, and monuments. I have noticed many of them throwing candy wrappers, cigarette butts, and other things on the ground, rather than in trash cans. It is rude for them to expect the people who live here to clean up after them.

I urge all tourists who visit our country to please be considerate of your hosts and to clean up after yourselves. That way we can all enjoy your visit.

Sincerely,
Sasha Pilcher

Send ➤

B **WRITING** Use your notes to write an e-mail letter to an international tourism website. Remember to state how you feel about the behavior and, if appropriate, how you would like behavior to change.

_____

_____

_____

_____

_____

_____

_____

_____

_____

_____

C **SELF-CHECK**

☐ Did I use the proper salutation and closing?

☐ Are the tone and language in my letter appropriate for the intended reader?

☐ Did I use regular spelling and punctuation and avoid abbreviations?

UNIT 6 Animals

PREVIEW

1 Complete the conversations with phrases from the box.

cooped up	in charge	put you in your place
feel sorry for	put up with	

1. **A:** I _____ the animals at the pet store.
   B: Why?
   A: They're _____ in the store all day.
   B: I know. But hopefully they'll find good homes soon.

2. **A:** The neighbor's dog is driving me crazy.
   B: Why? What's it doing?
   A: It barks all night. I can't _____ it any longer.

3. **A:** I tried to give Sara some advice on caring for her parrot, but she told me to mind my own business.
   B: Oh. I guess she _____.

4. **A:** How do your kids like the new puppy?
   B: They love him! But he needs to be trained; he doesn't obey us yet.
   A: Yes, you need to let him know that you're _____.

2 Match each animal with the adjective that best describes it. Write the letter on the line.

a. strong
b. quiet
c. brave
d. hairy
e. blind
f. slow
g. fat
h. cute

 1. _____ a bat

 2. _____ an ox

 3. _____ a mouse

 4. _____ a kitten

 5. _____ a lion

 6. _____ a pig

 7. _____ a gorilla

 8. _____ a snail

55

3 A simile is an expression that compares two things, using the words <u>like</u> or <u>as</u>.
Use your answers from Exercise 2 to write animal similes with <u>as</u>.

1. <u>as blind as a bat</u>

2. _____

3. _____

4. _____

5. _____

6. _____

7. _____

8. _____

4 Complete the sentence about yourself with a simile.

I'm _____.

Now use some of the similes from Exercise 3 to describe people you know,
famous people, or fictional characters.

1. <u>My boss is as blind as a bat.</u>

2. _____

3. _____

4. _____

5. _____

LESSON 1

5 Complete the sentences in the passive voice with <u>should</u> and a verb from the box.
Some verbs will be used more than once.

allow	give	keep	protect	provide	treat

1. Animals on large farms _____ humanely.

2. They _____ with healthy food.

3. They _____ with clean drinking water.

4. They _____ to interact with other animals.

5. The animals _____ space to move around.

6. They _____ from predators.

7. They _____ for illness or injury.

8. They _____ comfortable in extreme weather.

6 Complete the sentences with passive modals.

1. Dogfighting is illegal in all fifty U.S. states. Dogs _____ for fighting
   (can't / raise)
   in the United States.

2. Animals _____ for sport or entertainment. Hunting, animal fighting,
   (shouldn't / harm)
   animal racing, and use of animals in circuses should be illegal in all countries.

3. Animals _____ for their hides and fur. It's not necessary, because there are
(don't have to / kill)

so many man-made materials that can keep people just as warm.

4. The cruel practice of testing cosmetics on animals _____ if everyone buys
(can / eliminate)

only from companies that don't test on animals.

5. Pets _____ if there were more laws protecting them.
(might not / mistreat)

6. Alternatives to animal testing _____ in the next decade.
(might / develop)

7 What can be done to promote the humane treatment of animals? List some ideas.

_____

_____

LESSON **2**

8 **READING** Read about the advantages and disadvantages of owning different popular pets.

FINDING THE BEST PET FOR YOU
Take time to learn about the animal of your choice before bringing one home.

CATS

Cats are independent and easy pets to care for. And, as long as you aren't buying a purebred, they are economical pets, too.

Cats require little actual day-to-day care. They clean and groom themselves, tend to be self-reliant, and are usually happy to stay out of your way. But they can also be cuddly, playful, affectionate creatures—when they are interested.

Finding a kitten is usually easy, and they are often free.

DOGS

Dogs are generally eager to please, affectionate, loyal, and protective, but they demand lots of time and attention. They need plenty of exercise and thrive on interaction with their owners. Daily walks, frequent baths, and feeding are a must.

Dogs range in price from free to quite expensive for some breeds. If you decide to buy a purebred, research the various dog breeds to find the best match for your particular household.

RABBITS

Rabbits love to run, are very sociable and intelligent, and most are quite adorable.

When deciding whether a rabbit is the pet for you, keep in mind that they require daily attention and care, much like dogs. A rabbit should get lots of exercise, live in a dry spot in your home, and get time out of its cage.

Rabbits are not costly to purchase or care for, though it's important to keep fresh hay and leafy greens on hand for them to eat.

(continued on page 58)

HAMPSTERS

Hamsters are easy pets for practically any family. They are amusing, affable, and cute. Hamsters have simple needs and are cheap to buy and to keep.

Provide a dry living space outfitted with a gnawing log and a hiding place, and a hamster is content.

BIRDS

Birds have been blessed with lovely voices, though they are not quiet pets. Despite this, they are intelligent companions that are growing in popularity because they are pretty and quite independent.

Caring for birds is not difficult, but they do have special needs. They like to be active and to be challenged, and they must be housed in a place that is not too hot or too cold. Most love human interaction or other bird companions.

They should all be released from their cages periodically to explore their surroundings and to have the opportunity to fly.

Birds can be quite costly to purchase, depending on which bird you buy, but the cost of caring for a bird is quite low.

SNAKES

If you're the average person, this is not the pet you want. Snakes require careful attention and owners with special knowledge to care for them.

Before you buy a snake, consider that it may grow up to weigh twice what you do and refuse to eat anything but live animals such as mice or insects, which you will need to provide. Temperature and lighting must be controlled, and the snake's enclosure must be secure.

Snakes range from being placid and docile to aggressive, depending on the individual snake. They can be fairly costly to purchase and to maintain.

FISH

Fish fit well in almost any type of household. They're quiet, generally peaceful, and, depending on your tastes, not expensive to buy or to shelter. Care is relatively simple and involves monitoring water and food.

Usually, the biggest expense involves an aquarium, some of which can be very expensive. For those who do not want exotic, pricey fish, a simple, adequately built aquarium will do and costs much less.

Now complete the chart with information from the reading.

Pet	Personality traits	Care / special needs	Cost
Cats	independent, self-reliant	easy to care for	economical, often free
Dogs			
Rabbits			
Hamsters			
Birds			
Snakes			
Fish			

9 Use information from the chart in Exercise 8 to answer the following questions.

1. Which pets are low-maintenance?

   _____

2. Which pets are high-maintenance?

   _____

3. Which pets are costly to buy or care for?

   _____

4. Which pets are inexpensive to buy or care for?

   _____

5. Which pet would be best for your lifestyle? Explain.

   _____

   _____

Small dog breeds have become trendy in recent years. Celebrities such as Jessica Simpson and Lindsay Lohan are often spotted with their toy dogs tucked in their purses. As a result of this popularity, designer labels are selling high-end products for dogs—including clothes, collars, and jewelry.

LESSON 3

10 Complete the diagram to give examples of <u>Predators</u> and <u>Prey</u>. Use some animals from Student's Book page 62 and other animals that you know. List animals that can be both Predators and Prey where the circles overlap.

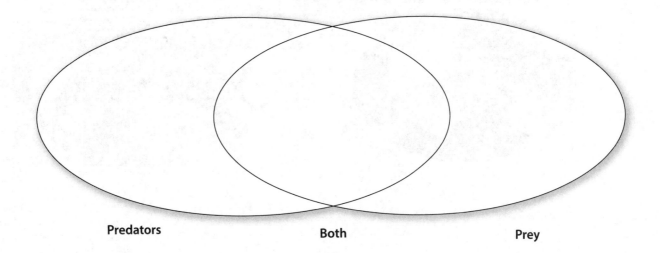

Predators   Both   Prey

11 Write sentences about three of the animals you listed in Exercise 10. What are their physical features? Do they form social groups? How do they hunt if they are predators? If they are prey, what do they do to protect themselves when they are threatened?

_____

_____

_____

_____

_____

_____

12 Look at the photos. What is each animal doing? Can you think of a similar human behavior? Complete the chart.

Animal behavior	Human behavior
1. Birds catch bugs and worms for their babies, bring them back to the nest, and feed the babies by putting the food in their beaks.	Humans make food for their babies and feed them with a bottle or a spoon.
2.	
3.	
4.	
5.	
6.	

13 **CHALLENGE** Expressions about animals are sometimes used to describe human behavior. Complete each expression with the correct animal.

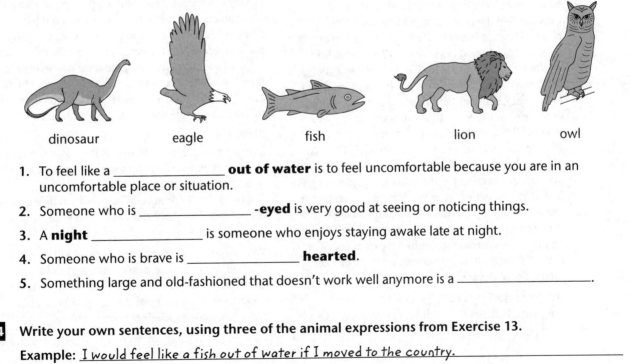

dinosaur   eagle   fish   lion   owl

1. To feel like a _____ **out of water** is to feel uncomfortable because you are in an uncomfortable place or situation.

2. Someone who is _____ -**eyed** is very good at seeing or noticing things.

3. A **night** _____ is someone who enjoys staying awake late at night.

4. Someone who is brave is _____ **hearted**.

5. Something large and old-fashioned that doesn't work well anymore is a _____.

14 Write your own sentences, using three of the animal expressions from Exercise 13.

Example: <u>I would feel like a fish out of water if I moved to the country.</u>

1. _____

2. _____

3. _____

15 READING Read the article.

The Death of a Lion Ignites Trophy Hunting Debate

In the summer of 2015, American dentist Walter Palmer went into hiding. Thousands of angry strangers were sending him and his family threatening messages via social media. Protestors appeared outside his office and home, waving signs calling him an evil murderer. What did Palmer do to set off this firestorm of negative attention? He went trophy hunting.

More specifically, Palmer participated in a hunting trip in the African country of Zimbabwe, during which he killed a lion. At the time, Palmer was unaware that the lion was a popular attraction at the nearby Hwange National Park, a protected game reserve. Nicknamed "Cecil," the 13-year-old lion was beloved by tourists for its unusual black mane and camera-friendly personality. Palmer also didn't know that Cecil was the subject of a 9-year wildlife conservation study run by Oxford University and wore a GPS collar that tracked its movements. Palmer, an avid big game hunter, spent $54,000 to hire local professional guides and to obtain a government hunting permit. After the guides illegally lured the lion out of the national park and onto private land, Palmer killed it, keeping the head and skin as a trophy. When news spread of Cecil's death, animal lovers across the world were outraged. The ethics of trophy hunting became a source of intense international debate.

Advocates insist that trophy hunting can bring long-term benefits for wildlife. For example, it's estimated that sport hunters spend over 2.9 billion dollars every year on permits and fees. This revenue can be used to fund conservation programs, establish national parks, and fight poachers who kill endangered animals illegally. Supporters also argue that the promise of income from hunters can motivate local landowners to support, rather than kill, endangered wildlife. When South Africa legalized the hunting of white rhinos, landowners reintroduced the species onto their properties, helping to increase the population from fewer than 100 to more than 11,000. Hunters also point out that they target only the largest animals—often males that are too old to reproduce. Removing these aggressive senior males can give younger males more access to the females, and more opportunities for the population to grow.

However, opponents of trophy hunting dispute these claims, arguing that little of the revenue generated by hunting is actually used for conservation. Rather, the money often disappears into the pockets of corrupt government officials. Critics also point out that responsible nature tourism generates significantly more revenue than trophy hunting. Studies from nine African countries show that hunting amounts to less than 2% of the total tourism revenue, a fact which clearly illustrates that tourists visit African countries to see and photograph wildlife, not kill it.

Furthermore, these reports estimate that only 3% of hunting revenue actually makes it back to the local communities where the hunting takes place. Finally, many animal lovers believe that it is our responsibility to protect endangered wildlife and that it's unethical to allow rich hunters to kill rare and beautiful animals for sport.

While Walter Palmer claims to regret killing Cecil the lion, it's clear that trophy hunting has become a controversial issue. Do we need to kill animals in order to save them? With strong opinions on both sides, the debate will likely continue.

Now answer the questions.

1. Why were people so angry at Walter Palmer? _____
   _____

2. What was special about Cecil? _____
   _____

3. What did Palmer's guides do that was illegal? _____
   _____

4. What effect did Palmer's actions have worldwide? _____
   _____

5. According to the supporters of trophy hunting, how does hunting benefit animal conservation?
   _____
   _____
   _____

6. What arguments do trophy hunting opponents make against the benefits you listed in item 5?
   _____
   _____
   _____
   _____

16 **WHAT DO YOU THINK? Answer the questions.**

1. Who do you think is more to blame for the killing of Cecil, a protected animal—Walter Palmer,
   or his guides? Explain your answer. _____
   _____
   _____

2. What is your opinion of the reactions to Palmer on social media? Were the reactions justified?
   _____
   _____

3. What is your opinion on trophy hunting? Which arguments from the article do you find
   most convincing? _____
   _____
   _____
   _____

According to many scientists, thousands of plant and animal species are at risk of extinction in the next few decades. One in three amphibians and a fifth of all mammals are threatened. Also, 68 percent of all plants are at risk of extinction.

GRAMMAR BOOSTER

A **Choose the modal that best completes each sentence.**

1. I _____ have a pet parrot, but they require too much care.

   a. had better   **b.** would like to   **c.** am able to   **d.** should

2. If you don't mind, I _____ eat out tonight.

   a. wouldn't   **b.** don't have to   **c.** would rather not   **d.** must not

3. _____ Hillary play the violin well?

   a. Should   **b.** Must   **c.** May   **d.** Can

4. I'm sorry, but I _____ come to the meeting tomorrow.

   a. must not   **b.** won't be able to   **c.** couldn't   **d.** don't have to

5. Your sister's a tennis player? She _____ be very athletic.

   a. must   **b.** could   **c.** should   **d.** may

6. We _____ go skiing this weekend. We haven't decided yet.

   a. shouldn't   **b.** can't   **c.** had better not   **d.** might not

7. You _____ feed the animals—it's against the rules!

   a. don't have to   **b.** might not   **c.** had better not   **d.** aren't able to

8. I _____ take this class. It's required.

   a. may   **b.** could   **c.** have to   **d.** can

B **Complete each sentence with a modal. More than one answer may be possible.**

1. You _____ turn on the TV while you wait, if you'd like.

2. It _____ snow tomorrow.

3. _____ I please borrow your pen for a moment?

4. If we leave at 4:00, there _____ be a lot of traffic.

5. We _____ check the weather before we go hiking.

6. If you don't want to see a movie, we _____ go out to eat instead.

7. My mother-in-law _____ have liked to go to Ireland, but she went to France instead.

8. He _____ have been very happy when he found out about his promotion.

9. You _____ smoke in this restaurant; it's prohibited.

10. He _____ come to the party last night because he had to work.

C **Complete each conversation in your own way. Use a modal.**

1. **A:** I passed Ellie on the street yesterday, and she didn't say hello.

   B: *She may not have seen you.*

2. **A:** It's too warm in here.

   B: _____

3. **A:** I don't feel like cooking tonight.

   B: _____

4. **A:** I don't know where to go on vacation this year.

   B: _____

5. **A:** Class was canceled yesterday.

   B: _____

6. **A:** I've had this cold for three weeks now.

   B: _____

7. **A:** I'm a little hungry.

   B: _____

8. **A:** My brother wants to get a pet.

   B: _____

A **PREWRITING: PLANNING YOUR ARGUMENT** Read the question below. State your opinion and list your arguments. Try to include examples, facts, or experts' opinions to support your opinion. Then list possible opposing arguments.

> *Is animal conservation important?*

Your opinion: _____

Your arguments	Possible opposing arguments
1. _____	1. _____
2. _____	2. _____
3. _____	3. _____

B **WRITING** Write a paragraph arguing your opinion from Exercise A. Remember to include a topic sentence at the beginning of the paragraph and a concluding sentence at the end.

_____
_____
_____
_____
_____
_____
_____
_____
_____
_____
_____
_____
_____

C **SELF-CHECK**

☐ Did I state my point of view clearly in the introduction?

☐ Did I provide examples, facts, or experts' opinions to support my point of view?

☐ Did I discuss opposing arguments?

☐ Did I include a concluding sentence?

Advertising and Consumers

1 Read the social media posts about shopping mistakes.

> We all make shopping mistakes once in a while. Are there any mistakes that you make regularly?
>
> View 4 more comments
>
> **Tia Marks**
> I'm a sucker for ads with celebrities in them. If I see a photo of a famous actress in a particular brand of clothing or makeup, then I suddenly want the same thing! It's crazy, I know. And expensive!
> Like • Reply • 1 hr 53 mins
>
> **Adam Baker**
> I guess you could say my problem is "keeping up with the Joneses." What I mean is this: If one of my friends gets a new phone or gadget, I feel like I need to go out and get one that's just as good or even better.
> Like • Reply • 1 hr 47 mins
>
> **Sandra Drummond**
> I can't pass up a good sale. There's something about getting a good deal, even if I don't need the product that's on sale. For example, last week a local store had a sale on back-packs, so I bought one. It's a really good backpack, and I got it for half price, but I don't need a backpack!
> Like • Reply • 1 hr 32 mins
>
> **Alex Smith**
> My problem is Internet shopping. It's so easy. When I'm bored, I start surfing the net, and often I end up buying something. And it's usually something I don't really need.
> Like • Reply • 1 hr 14 mins

Now describe each person's problem in your own words and write advice for each person.

1. Tia's problem: _____

   Your advice: _____

2. Adam's problem: _____

   Your advice: _____

3. Sandra's problem: _____

   Your advice: _____

4. Alex's problem: _____

   Your advice: _____

2 Complete the conversations with phrases from the box.

Don't fall for that.	Tell you what.
I could kick myself.	We'll call it even.
I owe you one.	You're comparing apples and oranges.

1. **A:** _____
   B: Why? What happened?

2. **A:** Look at this makeup. They say it will remove wrinkles!
   B: _____ There's no way that can be true.

3. **A:** My cat is much easier to take care of than my dog.
   B: They're very different types of pets. _____

4. **A:** I don't know if I can finish this report by the end of the day.
   B: _____ I don't have too much to do today. I'll lend you a hand.
   A: Thanks! _____

5. **A:** Thanks for helping me with my computer. How can I repay you?
   B: Oh, you've helped me many times. _____

LESSON 1

3 Read each statement and then suggest the best place for each person to shop in your city or town. Use the vocabulary from Student's Book page 76.

I want to pick up some cheap sunglasses. It would be a waste of money to buy designer ones. I'd just lose them!

I'd like to get some coffee, take a walk in this beautiful weather, and check out the new fall fashions.

1. *The open-air market on Fifth Street is a good place for bargain hunting.*
   _____

2. _____
   _____
   _____

I've been saving up for a new digital camera. I'd like to check out a couple of different places before I buy one.

I don't really need anything, but I wouldn't mind just looking around. I actually find shopping relaxing.

3. _____
   _____
   _____

4. _____
   _____
   _____

4 Look online for something you're interested in buying. Record the prices you find on different websites. Comment on shipping costs, available brands, customer service, etc.

What are you shopping for? _____

Any particular brand? _____

Website: _____
Price: _____
Comments: _____
_____

Website: _____
Price: _____
Comments: _____
_____

Which website had the best buy?

_____

Website: _____
Price: _____
Comments: _____
_____

5 **READING** Read the advice on shopping in Tokyo. Then complete the statements and answer the questions on page 70.

TOKYO SHOPPING GUIDE Below are descriptions of some of the best places to shop in Tokyo.

SOUVENIRS

"100-Yen" Shops
You can find 100-yen shops around many train stations and in some shopping areas. 100-yen shops are stores where most items cost 100 yen or less. In 100-yen shops, you can buy chopsticks, tableware, fans, kites, origami paper, calligraphy sets, "Hello Kitty" items, and much, much more! If you're looking for cheap souvenirs, 100-yen shops are the places to go.

Nakamise Shopping Arcade
This colorful, lively outdoor shopping street leads to the oldest temple in Tokyo. The walkway has been lined with souvenir shops and local food

stands for centuries. You'll find paper umbrellas, kimonos, rice cakes, sweets, and much more. Prices are, for the most part, reasonable.

Oriental Bazaar
Oriental Bazaar is the largest and most famous souvenir shop in Tokyo. It has four floors, and the higher you go, the more expensive the items get. Here you can satisfy all of your gift-giving needs at reasonable prices.

ELECTRONICS

Akihabara
Looking for the latest electronic gadgets? Check out the Akihabara district. It's the place to find the newest cell phones, TVs, manga anime videos and computer games, and even miniature robot pets.

CLOTHING AND ACCESSORIES

Ginza
The Ginza is a famous high-end shopping district in Tokyo. It's full of upscale department stores and expensive designer boutiques. The fashions tend to be more conservative here. For younger and trendier styles, go to Shibuya or Harajuku.

1. _____ are the best places to find inexpensive souvenirs in Tokyo.

2. If you're interested in the latest technology, you might want to check out _____.

3. At _____, you might find a plastic samurai sword that's a steal in the basement and a traditional kimono that's a good deal on the top floor.

4. Prices are a bit steep here. If you're looking for a bargain, _____ is probably not the place to shop.

5. To pick up a few souvenirs, try some local snacks, and do a little sightseeing at the same time, _____ is a good bet.

   _____

6. Where would you like to shop? Why? _____

LESSON 2

6 Think of something that happened to you or that you heard about recently that blew you away, got on your nerves, cracked you up, or choked you up. What was it? Why did it make you feel that way?

_____

_____

7 Complete each sentence with a passive gerund or infinitive. Use verbs from the box.

ask	entertain	ignore	treat
call	force	inform	

1. Alex can't stand _____ by telemarketers.

2. I enjoy _____ by funny commercials.

3. We hate _____ to watch ads before movies.

4. I appreciate _____ to join this company.

5. Scott hates _____.

6. Pam doesn't want _____ about new products.

7. My daughter dislikes _____ like a baby.

8 How do you feel about these forms of advertising? Write sentences with passive gerunds or infinitives. Use verbs from the box or your own verbs.

can't stand	don't appreciate	like	prefer
dislike	don't like	love	resent

1. Spam: _I don't appreciate being sent e-mail ads that I don't want._____

2. Ads before movies: _____

3. Internet ads: _____

4. Direct mail: _____

5. Telemarketing calls: _____

6. Magazine ads: _____

7. Free product samples: _____

8. Product placement in movies: _____

9 **READING WARM-UP** Answer the questions.

1. Do you enjoy shopping? _____

2. Do you feel comfortable shopping alone? _____

3. How often do you go shopping? _____

4. What do you buy for yourself? _____

5. Do you see a difference between men's and women's attitudes toward shopping?

_____

10 **READING** Read about the shopping habits of North American men. Then answer the questions on page 72.

Shift in Men's Shopping Habits

According to recent studies, the shopping habits of men are changing significantly. In contrast to the traditional image of men as unwilling shoppers who aren't comfortable shopping for their own clothes, the new findings suggest that men now shop as a leisure activity, and that they make more impulse purchases of clothing than in the past.

Men are becoming independent and more confident shoppers. They're well-informed, willing to shop alone, and they are increasingly doing their clothing shopping online, comparing prices on retail websites, and making their own style decisions. Men are also paying more attention to fashion and are much more willing to experiment with style and splurge on fashion items than in the past.

In addition, the study found that men shop more often than in the past and are increasingly likely to buy certain products for themselves — especially electronics, casual clothing, watches, and fragrance or grooming products.

Unfortunately, shopping is almost as likely to become an addiction for men as it is for women. According to some estimates, about 6% of women and 5.5% of men are compulsive shoppers.

Among the findings of the studies:
- Men spend on average US $10 more per month on clothing than women do.
- Men prefer shopping on their phones: 45% of men shop for clothing on their phones, whereas 34% of women do.
- Women are much more likely to pay attention to sales than men are: 74% of women buy sale items online versus 54% of men.
- A luxury men's fashion shopping site says that its busiest days are Tuesdays and Fridays, when some famous luxury brands add new items to their website.
- The average age of male apparel shoppers is 30–39.

Now answer the questions.

1. According to the study, how are the shopping habits of men changing?

   _____

   _____

2. Do you think men's shopping habits are changing in a similar way in your country?
   Give examples to explain your answer.

   _____

   _____

3. Do you think the shift in men's shopping habits described in the article is a positive or
   a negative development? Explain your answer.

   _____

   _____

11 **READING WARM-UP** Answer the questions.

1. What country do you think does the most online shopping? _____

2. What do you think is the most popular online purchase? _____

12 **READING** Read about Internet shopping habits.

Trends in Online Shopping

According to recent surveys, more than 1.4 billion people have shopped online. Clothing and accessories were the most popular purchase, with over 50% of people indicating that they intended to purchase clothing online in the next six months. Purchases of clothing were followed closely by airline tickets and hotel reservations, event tickets, books (both hard copy and e-books), and personal care products.

Among the 30,000 people in 60 countries who were surveyed, people in Asia were the world's most frequent online shoppers, with 41–59% of respondents making online purchases. Asian shoppers were followed by those in Europe and the Middle East / Africa, while U.S. and Latin American shoppers made the fewest online purchases.

Online shoppers can also be broken down by age. The age group making the most online purchases worldwide is people ages 21–34, with 52–63% making purchases online. Following them are people ages 35–49, with 25–30% making online purchases. Most online shoppers preferred to use computers, though cell phone purchases are becoming increasingly popular worldwide, especially in Asia.

Why do global consumers shop online? One of the main attractions of Internet shopping is its convenience. Another feature of online shopping that is important to people is the ability to compare prices across many online retail sites. A final compelling reason given by a high percentage of respondents is simply that online shopping is fun.

In countries with widespread Internet access, some reasons people give for *not* shopping online include the expense of surfing, nervousness about using credit cards online, worries about companies collecting information about their shopping tastes, and reluctance to purchase goods from retailers they don't know.

Now answer the questions.

1. Were you surprised by the most popular online purchase? _____

2. Why do you think people buy more clothing than any other product online? _____
_____

3. Why do you think more people use computers rather than cell phones for online shopping? Do you
think this will change in the future? _____
_____

4. Do any of the concerns about online shopping worry you? Why or why not? _____
_____

13 Complete the chart by listing some advantages and disadvantages of shopping online.

Advantages	Disadvantages
It's easier to comparison shop.	

14 Check the items that you have purchased online.

- ☐ clothing / accessories / shoes
- ☐ hotel reservations or tour bookings
- ☐ music downloads
- ☐ books

- ☐ airline tickets
- ☐ event tickets
- ☐ electronic devices
- ☐ personal care products

Now circle the items you've purchased in the last month. How many online purchases
do you think you've made in the last month? _____

15 **Answer the questions.**

1. Describe consumer shopping habits in your country—including online shopping. Do you see differences between older and younger shoppers? Between women and men?

   _____

   _____

   _____

2. Describe your own shopping habits. Are you a compulsive shopper? Do you ever indulge yourself? How often? Do you ever make impulse buys, or do you wait and shop when there is a sale?

   _____

   _____

   _____

LESSON 4

16 **Complete each sentence with a word from the box.**

endorse	imply	promote	prove

> In 1991, the Swedish government banned advertising directed at children under the age of twelve.

1. My kids are really going to want to get their hands on those sneakers now that their favorite baseball player has agreed to _____ them.

2. I would buy the more expensive brand of toothpaste if the company could _____ that it's more effective at fighting cavities.

3. I heard First Choice Pizza is giving away free slices tonight to _____ its chain of restaurants.

4. The ads _____ that their competitor's cars are unsafe.

17 **Look again at the list of advertising techniques on Student's Book page 82. Can you think of ads that use these techniques? Complete the chart for as many of the techniques as you can.**

Advertising technique	Product	How the technique is used
Example: Provide facts and figures	ZX-10 MP3 player	The manufacturer states how many songs it holds, how little it weighs, and how many hours it can play.
1. Provide facts and figures		
2. Convince people to "jump on the bandwagon"		
3. Play on people's hidden fears		

Advertising technique	Product	How the technique is used
4. Play on people's patriotism		
5. Provide "snob appeal"		
6. Associate positive qualities with a product		
7. Provide testimonials		
8. Manipulate people's emotions		

Which of these techniques do you think is most effective? Why? _____

_____

GRAMMAR BOOSTER

A **Rewrite each sentence in the passive voice.**

1. Retailers all over the world sell our products.

   _____

2. Scott Joplin wrote that song.

   _____

3. Online stores are selling those shoes at a steep discount.

   _____

4. Jason Farah is going to endorse the new line of running shoes.

   _____

5. By the time we get to the concert hall, people will have taken all the good seats.

   _____

6. An ad that provides facts and figures can persuade Stu.

   _____

7. CompTech has hired Ella to design its website.

   _____

8. City Symphony is going to perform a new opera tonight.

   _____

B Rewrite each of your sentences from Exercise A as a <u>yes</u> / <u>no</u> question.

1. _____
2. _____
3. _____
4. _____
5. _____
6. _____
7. _____
8. _____

C Complete each question in the passive voice.

1. **A:** When _____?
   B: Our house was built in 1920.

2. **A:** What time _____?
   B: Lunch will be served at 12:30.

3. **A:** How long _____?
   B: We were given 2 hours to complete the test.

4. **A:** Where _____?
   B: The party will be held at City Hall.

5. **A:** _____?
   B: No, she's not being given an award tonight.

6. **A:** _____ yet?
   B: No, the house hasn't been sold yet.

Choose one of the following articles to summarize:

- *Bird-poop Facials*, Workbook page 39–40
- *Questionable Cosmetic Treatments*, Student's Book page 44
- *The Will to Make a Difference*, Student's Book page 70
- An article you've read outside of class

A **PREWRITING: IDENTIFYING MAIN IDEAS** Read the article you've chosen and underline or highlight the important parts. Then read the article again and list the main ideas below. (The article you have chosen may have fewer than six paragraphs.)

Main idea of paragraph 1:
Main idea of paragraph 2:
Main idea of paragraph 3:
Main idea of paragraph 4:
Main idea of paragraph 5:
Main idea of paragraph 6:

B **WRITING** Combine the main ideas to write your summary. Be sure to paraphrase what the author says, using your own words. Your summary should have one or two sentences for every paragraph in the original article.

_____

_____

_____

_____

_____

_____

_____

_____

_____

_____

_____

_____

_____

_____

Reporting verbs:
argue	point out
believe	report
conclude	state
explain	

Common expressions:
According to _____,
In _____'s opinion,
As _____ explains,
From _____'s point of view,

C **SELF-CHECK**

☐ Does the summary include only the author's main ideas?

☐ Did I paraphrase the author's ideas?

☐ Was I careful not to include my opinion in the summary?

1 Read each situation. Then complete each sentence summarizing what happened. Use the expressions from the box and your own words. One of the situations will use two expressions.

behind her back	~~have a falling out~~	split up
fall apart	hit the nail on the head	
going downhill	patch things up	

1. Tina and her sister Marie had a big fight last month. They weren't speaking to each other for a few weeks. But I just heard that they got together and talked and worked everything out. Now they're just as close as they were before. I'm so glad.

   Tina and Marie _____*had a falling out*_____, but then _____.

2. Sara is coming to the party, but Gary isn't. I heard that they're not together any more. It's really too bad.

   Sara and Gary _____.

3. Did you hear that Jason just quit his job? He got a new boss earlier this year, and I guess things at the office just started getting worse and worse. Finally, Jason had enough and couldn't take anymore.

   _____, and finally Jason quit his job.

4. I was wondering why they hadn't arrived yet, but I think you're exactly right, Tom — they must be stuck in traffic.

   Tom _____.

5. Jan and Mike were going to buy an apartment in the city. But at the last minute, the people who were selling the apartment decided not to sell.

   Jan and Mike were going to buy an apartment, but then _____.

6. Marsha told me that she doesn't like Peggy. It made me uncomfortable to hear that she thought Peggy was selfish.

   Marsha _____.

2 How can parents raise well-behaved kids who won't turn into troublemakers? Write sentences using <u>should</u> or <u>shouldn't</u>.

Should	Shouldn't
Kids should be given clear rules to follow.	Kids shouldn't be criticized constantly.

3 Rewrite each sentence with a repeated comparative so that the sentence describes a trend. (Some sentences can be rewritten more than one way.)

1. People are moving to cities to find work.

   More and more people are moving to cities to find work.

2. People are spending long hours at work.

   People are spending longer and longer hours at work.

3. Men are getting involved in caring for their children.

   _____

4. People are spending time with their extended families.

   _____

5. Mothers are staying home to take care of their children.

   _____

6. Couples are choosing to remain childless.

   _____

7. Young adults are moving out of their parents' homes.

   _____

8. Adolescents receive adult supervision.

   _____

4 Complete the sentences, using double comparatives. Use the correct form of each word from the box.

develop	few	good	less	low	more

1. _____ people work, _____ time they spend with their families.

2. _____ a country is, _____ the healthcare system.

3. _____ the birthrate, _____ children there will be to care for older members of society.

few	good	high	long	more	old

4. _____ education you have, _____ your salary will be.

5. _____ the health-care system, _____ people live.

6. _____ people are when they get married, _____ children they are likely to have.

> According to a study by the United Nations, by the middle of the 21st century the birth rate in 139 countries will not be high enough to replace the existing population.

5 Complete each double comparative. Use your own ideas.

1. The longer I live, _____.

2. The harder you work, _____.

3. The more that you read, _____.

4. The better I get to know people, _____.

5. The more things change, _____.

Now compare your sentences with these famous quotes.

> "The longer I live, the more beautiful life becomes."
> —Frank Lloyd Wright, architect (1869–1959)

> "The harder you work, the luckier you get."
> —Samuel Goldwyn, movie producer (1882–1974)

> "The more that you read, the more things you will know. The more that you learn, the more places you'll go."
> —Dr. Seuss, children's book author (1904–1991)

> "The better I get to know men, the more I find myself loving dogs."
> —Charles De Gaulle, French leader (1890–1970)

> "The more things change, the more they are the same."
> —Alphonse Karr, author (1808–1890)

Choose one of the quotes and describe what it means. How does it apply to your life and/or to the world today?

_____

_____

_____

LESSON 2

6 What do you think parents should do if their teenaged kids start smoking?
Read each idea and decide how effective you think it would be.

Parents should . . .	ineffective	somewhat effective	very effective
accept that there's not much they can do.	○	○	○
talk to their kids about the health risks of smoking.	○	○	○
ask their kids questions to find out why they are smoking.	○	○	○
ground them.	○	○	○
let their kids know that they disapprove of their smoking.	○	○	○
talk to their kids about other negative effects of smoking, such as poor sports performance, smelly clothes and hair, bad breath, and yellow teeth.	○	○	○
allow their kids to make their own mistakes.	○	○	○
explain how the tobacco industry's advertising targets young people to become smokers.	○	○	○

(continued)

Parents should . . .	ineffective	somewhat effective	very effective
have their kids visit people who have lung cancer.	○	○	○
not make a big deal about a little bit of rebellious behavior.	○	○	○
quit smoking themselves if they are smokers.	○	○	○

What do you think is the best idea? Why? _____

_____

7 **Read the teen blog entries and describe the teens' or their parents' behavior. Use the vocabulary from Student's Book page 90.**

💬 Comment   ➜ Share

1. Posted: 10:09 AM
Princess5574
Hey! It's my birthday! When I woke up this morning, I went downstairs and opened the gifts my parents had left for me. I got some jewelry, some clothes, a new laptop — nothing special. I was a little disappointed. But when I walked out of the house, I found my real present in the driveway! My sports car — exactly the one I had asked for. I can't wait to drive it to my party on Saturday. REPLY

2. Posted: 11:48 AM
Nolife312
They gave you a car? My parents won't even let me learn how to drive, or go anywhere in anyone else's car – or ride my bike down the street! They're afraid I'll hurt myself, I guess. I need to be able to hang out with my friends, go to the movies, maybe even go to a party every once in a while. I love my parents, but they're ruining my life! REPLY

3. Posted: 1:02 PM
Norules721
Well, at least your parents care about what you do. My parents let me go where I want, do what I want. They don't mind if I invite the whole school over for a party. I know they love me, but I wish they would stop trying to be "cool" and act more like parents. REPLY

4. Posted: 1:34 PM
Noworries219
My parents set rules about everything. From the moment I get up, they watch every move I make and put restrictions on everything. But I don't care. I do what I want. If I want to go to a party, and they say I can't, I just sneak out and go anyway! REPLY

1. *Princess is spoiled. Her parents are* _____

2. _____

3. _____

4. _____

8 **WHAT ABOUT YOU?** Check the sentences that describe your upbringing.

Lenient upbringing	Strict upbringing
⚪ My parents did things for me that I could or should have done for myself.	⚪ My parents made me do many things for myself.
⚪ My parents did not expect me to do many chores or to help much around the house.	⚪ I had to do a lot of chores around the house.
⚪ I was allowed to have almost any clothes I wanted.	⚪ I had to use my own money to buy clothes.
⚪ My parents gave me too much freedom.	⚪ I wasn't given very much freedom.
⚪ My parents allowed me to take the lead or dominate the family.	⚪ My parents used physical punishment to discipline me.
⚪ My parents did not enforce their rules.	⚪ My parents set a lot of rules for me to follow.

Do you think you were spoiled as a child? Were your parents too strict? Or did you grow up with a nice balance between strictness and leniency? Explain and try to give examples.

_____

_____

_____

What should parents do (or not do) to raise kids who aren't spoiled? List some ideas.

_____

_____

_____

LESSON 3

9 Match the words with their definitions. Write the letter on the line.

1. _____ frustration

2. _____ involvement

3. _____ courtesy

4. _____ maturity

5. _____ obedience

a. willingness to do what someone in a position of authority tells you to do

b. the quality of behaving in a sensible way and like an adult

c. the act of taking part in an activity or event, or the way in which you take part in it

d. the feeling of being annoyed, upset, or impatient because you cannot control or change a situation or achieve something

e. polite behavior that shows that you have respect for other people

10 **CHALLENGE** **Choose the best word to complete each sentence.**

1. His parents intend for him to get married as soon as he finishes college. That is their _____.

   a. explanation   **b.** importance   **c.** expectation   **d.** impatience

2. Carl Brooks is almost thirty-eight years old and still living in his parents' home. His parents resent his _____.

   a. dependence   **b.** dependability   **c.** development   **d.** difference

3. Her parents don't think she should change jobs again. They worry about her long-term financial _____.

   a. mobility   **b.** security   **c.** lenience   **d.** confidence

4. Dana Wolf doesn't like her daughter's new boyfriend. She thinks he's lazy and disrespectful. She can't understand her daughter's _____ to him.

   a. attractiveness   **b.** consideration   **c.** involvement   **d.** attraction

5. The company's _____ improved after they hired three new employees.

   a. productive   **b.** maturity   **c.** productivity   **d.** responsibility

11 **Answer the questions.**

1. What is a "generation gap"?

   _____

2. What developments (political, technological, social, etc.) do you think have contributed to the generation gap between your generation and that of your parents?

   _____

   _____

3. In what ways are your generation and that of your parents similar?

   _____

   _____

LESSON 4

12 **READING WARM-UP** How are the responsibilities of caring for children different from those of caring for the elderly? How are they the same?

_____

_____

_____

_____

The Sandwich Generation

In the United States and Canada they've been termed the sandwich generation—people caught between the needs of their growing children and their aging parents, having to care for both. Factors giving rise to the sandwich generation include the fact that people are having children later in life, combined with longer life expectancies. Whatever the cause, this new responsibility places many demands on these caregivers' time and energy and leaves little space for attending to their own needs.

Some members of the sandwich generation are parents in their 30s or 40s caring for young children. For example, Pamela Bose, 40, has a three-year-old and a nine-year-old. She has recently taken over the care of her widowed mother. One minute she is worrying about getting the children to school on time; the next, she is checking to make sure that her mother has remembered to take her medicine. "I spend so much time keeping up with their competing demands that I end up not devoting enough time to anyone, let alone making time for myself," says Bose.

Other members of the sandwich generation are parents in their 40s or 50s caring for teenaged or adult children. Nowadays, more adult children are living at home while they're in college and even afterward, as they get established and figure out what they want to do. Also, an increasing number of adult children are returning home to live after a divorce or job loss.

The longer adult children remain dependent on their parents, the more people find themselves in the sandwich generation. Patricia Rivas is one of these people. She and her husband David both have careers. They have a teenaged son, a recently divorced daughter with a two-year-old child, and an elderly father who has early dementia and is requiring more and more care, all living in the same household.

Most sandwich-generation caregivers are women. Increased female labor-force participation means that many of these women are balancing not only care for their children and parents but also their own careers. Without a doubt, trying to meet all of these obligations at the same time is stressful. It's not surprising that sandwich-generation members report an increase in depression, sleeplessness, headaches, and other health problems. While many are happy about the chance to help care for their parents, they also feel guilty about not doing more.

As sandwich-generation members try to respond to everyone else's needs, it's important that they not ignore their own needs. As these caregivers struggle to give their young children attention and patience, their older children support and guidance, their elderly parents physical care and opportunities for social interaction and inclusion in family life, it is also important that they make some time for their own relaxation. Unfortunately, such relaxation is more often than not overlooked.

Now answer the questions.

1. What is the "sandwich generation"?

_____

2. How is the term "sandwich" appropriate to describe this generation?

_____

3. Name three trends that are responsible for the development of the "sandwich generation."

_____

_____

_____

4. What are some problems that sandwich-generation members experience?

_____

_____

5. Why is being a member of the sandwich generation especially stressful for women?

_____

_____

14 **Look back at the article in Exercise 13. Find the nouns that correspond to the verbs and adjectives below. Write them on the lines.**

1. responsible: _____

2. participate: _____

3. obligate: _____

4. depress: _____

5. sleepless: _____

6. patient: _____

7. guide: _____

8. interact: _____

9. include: _____

10. relax: _____

> Life expectancy in the People's Republic of China was around 40 years in the middle of the 20th century. By 2010, it had risen to around 75 years.

> In the U.S., approximately 47 percent of people between the ages of 45 and 55 have children under 21 and also have aging parents or in-laws.

15 **Do you know anyone who is caring for his or her children and/or an elderly family member? Describe the person's situation. What challenges is he or she facing?**

A Read each pair of statements. Then complete each sentence, using a comparative, superlative, or comparison with <u>as . . . as</u>.

1. Today's hike is 5 km. But our hike yesterday was 7 km.

   Today's hike is *shorter than yesterday's hike* _____.

2. A cheetah can run 96 km per hour. A greyhound can run 64 km per hour.

   A greyhound can't run _____.

3. I am 24 years old. My brother is 20, and my sister is 18.

   Of the three of us, I am _____.

4. Park City is 5 km from here. Greenville is 10 km from here.

   Greenville is _____.

5. His parents are very strict. My parents are not very strict.

   My parents are _____.

6. Mr. Plant has two children. Mr. Lane has four children.

   Mr. Plant has _____.

7. I paint well. Ten years ago, I didn't paint well.

   I paint _____.

8. There are five people in my family. There are five people in Irene Lee's family, too.

   There are _____.

9. My commute to work is 14 km. My colleague Mrs. Young has a 20 km commute, and my other colleague, Mr. Davis, travels 30 km to work.

   Of the three of us, I have _____.

10. My grandmother is 80 years old. My grandfather is 78 years old.

    My grandfather isn't _____.

11. When Nina was younger, she needed ten hours of sleep each night. Now she is a teenager, and she needs only eight hours of sleep each night.

    Now that Nina is a teenager, she needs _____.

B Compare people and things you know. Use comparatives or __as__ . . . __as__.

Example: two friends — adventurous

Megan is more adventurous than Matthew.

1. two friends — adventurous

_____

2. two movies — funny

_____

3. two books — long

_____

4. two stores — expensive

_____

5. two TV shows — good

_____

6. two singers — sing well

_____

7. two family members — work hard

_____

C Complete each statement. Use your own idea in the first blank and a superlative in the second.

1. ___Liver___ is _the worst_ thing I've ever eaten.

2. _____ is _____ person I've ever met.

3. _____ is _____ place I've ever been.

4. _____ is _____ thing I've ever done.

5. _____ is _____ thing I've ever bought.

6. _____ is _____ thing I've ever said.

D **CHALLENGE** Read each sentence. Then write a sentence with similar meaning, using a comparative, a superlative, or __as__ . . . __as__.

1. At 421 meters, the Jin Mao Building in Shanghai is very tall.

   The Jin Mao Building in Shanghai is more than 400 meters tall.

2. The population of Greenland is only 56,238.

   _____

3. The movie we watched last night was so depressing.

   _____

4. Alexis McCarthy is becoming a very good violin player because she practices daily.

   _____

5. Sometimes he watches TV, but usually he reads.

   _____

6. The new French restaurant on City Avenue looks expensive, but it's really not.

   _____

A **PREWRITING: COMPARE & CONTRAST CHART** Choose a family member of a different generation from you. Write his or her name in the box next to "ME." Then fill in the chart with how your generations are similar and how they are different.

COMPARING GENERATIONS

ME	_____

Similarities

Differences	

B **WRITING** Write one or two paragraphs comparing the two generations you chose. Include a topic sentence that expresses your main idea. Avoid run-on sentences and comma splices.

_____
_____
_____
_____
_____
_____
_____
_____
_____
_____

C **SELF-CHECK**

☐ Did I avoid run-on sentences and comma splices?

☐ Do all the sentences support the topic sentence?

☐ Did I use the vocabulary and expressions I learned in this unit?

UNIT

9

PREVIEW

Facts, Theories, and Hoaxes

1 **Read the stories below. Rate the probability that each is true.**

1.   A couple was on vacation in Australia, driving through the bush, when they accidentally hit a kangaroo. They decided to prop the kangaroo up and take a photo. To add a bit of humor, they dressed it up in the husband's jacket.

   As it turned out, the kangaroo was only stunned, not dead, and it hopped away with the jacket on. In the jacket pocket were the keys to their rental car and all their vacation money.

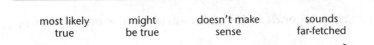

most likely true   might be true   doesn't make sense   sounds far-fetched

2.   A college student stayed up late studying for a math final exam. He overslept and arrived late for the test. He found three problems written on the board. He solved the first two pretty easily but struggled with the third. He worked frantically and figured out a solution just before the time was up.

   That night the student received a phone call from his professor, who told him that the third problem wasn't a test question. Before the test had started, the professor had explained that it was a problem previously thought to be unsolvable. But the student had solved it!

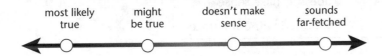

most likely true   might be true   doesn't make sense   sounds far-fetched

3.   A man was jogging through the park one day when another jogger lightly bumped him and excused himself. The man was just a little annoyed—until he realized that his wallet was missing. He immediately began chasing the jogger who'd bumped into him. He caught up to him and tackled him, yelling, "Give me that wallet!" The frightened "thief" handed over a wallet and quickly ran off.

   When the man got home, his wife asked him if he'd remembered to stop at the store. Anxious to tell his story, the man said that he hadn't, but that he had a good excuse. Before he finished, his wife said, "I know—you left your wallet on the dresser."

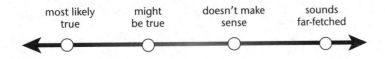

most likely true   might be true   doesn't make sense   sounds far-fetched

2 Now put the conversation about the third story on the previous page in order. Write numbers on the lines.

_____ What? You've heard it before?

_____ What happened?

_____ It's a story that people pass on, about something unusual that happened to an ordinary person. A lot of people believe them, but they're usually not true.

__1__ You'll never guess what happened to a friend of a friend's husband.

_____ Yeah, I have. The jogger took the other guy's wallet and then got home and realized he had left his wallet at home. It's an urban legend.

_____ Wow. I had no idea. It seemed believable.

_____ Well, he was jogging in the park, and this guy bumped into him. He thought the guy had stolen his wallet, so he chased him and tackled him . . .

_____ What's an urban legend?

_____ Don't tell me you buy that story!

3 CHALLENGE Do you know any urban legends or fantastic stories? Write one of them in your own words.

_____

_____

_____

_____

_____

_____

4 Complete the conversation with phrases from the box.

going out on a limb	doesn't make sense
barking up the wrong tree	vanished without a trace

A: My wallet is missing. It was in my purse, but it seems to have _____. Someone at the party must have taken it.

B: Hmm. I think you're _____.

A: What do you mean?

B: It _____. You know almost everyone who was at the party. I may be _____ here, but I think you probably just misplaced it.

A: You're probably right.

5 Complete the conversations. Speculate about the situations, using vocabulary from Student's Book page 100.

1. A: My dad was supposed to meet me after school at 3:30. It's 4:05, and he's still not here.

   B: _____

2. A: Lisa was supposed to call me half an hour ago. I wonder why she hasn't called.

   B: _____

3. A: My dog usually loves going for walks, but today she won't even come outside with me. What do you think could be wrong?

   B: _____

4. A: Usually the sanitation department picks up the trash on Monday mornings. It's 4 P.M., and they still haven't picked up the trash on my street.

   B: _____

5. A: I bought tickets to see the Velvet Overboards in concert this weekend. I was really excited, but I just heard that they cancelled the concert. I have no idea why.

   B: _____

6. A: The new employee was supposed to start today, but he hasn't come to work. I wonder what happened?

   B: _____

6 Read the situation below. Then, for each of the times listed, write a sentence about what could have happened. Use vocabulary from Student's Book page 100.

CENTRAL STATION

Your friend was supposed to arrive on the 8:05 train. You are waiting outside the station, but she still isn't there.

Example: (8:10) Not certain: _Maybe she's getting her luggage._

1. (8:10) Not certain: _____

2. (8:20) Almost certain: _____

3. (8:35) Very certain: _____

7 **Rewrite the sentences with perfect modals in the active voice.**

1. Clearly, the ancient Greeks didn't build an underwater city.

   The ancient Greeks couldn't have built an underwater city.

2. Most likely people used the statues for religious ceremonies.

   _____

3. The Egyptians who built the pyramids probably used sleds to move large blocks of stone.

   _____

4. Those patterns in the earth were definitely not made by aliens.

   _____

5. It's possible that a storm caused all this damage.

   _____

6. Clearly, this was an important place for the early inhabitants.

   _____

8 **Read each statement and check whether each speaker is <u>very certain</u>, <u>almost certain</u>, or <u>not certain</u>. Then rewrite each sentence, using a perfect modal in the passive voice. Use the appropriate degree of certainty.**

very certain   almost certain   not certain

1. ☐ ☐ ☑ It's possible that language was initially developed to allow humans to hunt in groups more effectively.

   Language may have been developed to allow humans to hunt in groups more effectively.

2. ☐ ☐ ☐ Maybe the dinosaurs were killed by climate changes.

   _____

3. ☐ ☐ ☐ Probably the giant stone statues on Easter Island were carved by the ancestors of the Polynesian people who live there today.

   _____

4. ☐ ☐ ☐ Most likely Amelia Earhart was killed when her plane ran out of fuel and went down in the Pacific Ocean.

   _____

5. ☐ ☐ ☐ Clearly, the fire was started intentionally.

   _____

6. ☐ ☐ ☐ There's no question the ship was sunk by a collision with an iceberg.

   _____

9 **READING WARM-UP** Look at the picture and caption. Then speculate about what happened to the *Mary Celeste,* using the perfect form of the modal <u>may</u> in the passive voice.

Example: *The crew may have been washed overboard by a giant wave.*

Your speculation: _____

_____

THE MARY CELESTE. DECEMBER 5TH, 1872.

The *Mary Celeste* was discovered drifting off the coast of Portugal in 1872. There was no one aboard.

10 **READING** Read more about the circumstances surrounding the disappearance of the *Mary Celeste's* crew and passengers.

The Mary Celeste

On November 7, 1872, the *Mary Celeste* sailed under the command of Captain Benjamin Briggs—known as an honest and fair man. He, his wife, young daughter, and a crew of seven departed from New York City for Genoa, Italy, carrying a cargo of alcohol. They were never seen again.

On December 4, another ship spotted the *Mary Celeste* drifting off the coast of Portugal. A few men from the ship boarded the *Mary Celeste* to offer help. Although there was some damage, it was not extensive, and the ship was seaworthy. The cargo and a six-month supply of food and water were still on board the ship. However, nine of the 1,700 barrels of alcohol were empty, and the lifeboat and all of the passengers and crew were missing. The last entry in the logbook was dated November 24, 1872.

Many theories have been proposed to explain the mystery of the disappearance of the *Mary Celeste's* crew and passengers. Here are some of them:

• The crew killed Captain Briggs and his family and escaped in the lifeboat.

• The nine barrels of alcohol had leaked. Afraid the fumes would cause an explosion, Captain Briggs ordered everyone into the lifeboat. The lifeboat got separated from the ship, and its occupants drowned or died at sea.

• A giant octopus snatched the crew one by one from the deck of the ship.

Now speculate about the probability of each theory explaining the disappearance of the *Mary Celeste's* passengers and crew. Use perfect modals in the passive voice. Explain your answers.

1. The theory that the captain was killed by the crew:

_____

_____

2. The theory that the crew was forced by alcohol fumes to leave the ship:

_____

_____

3. The theory that the crew was snatched from the ship by a giant octopus:

_____

_____

11 Complete the paragraph, using <u>believable</u>, <u>debatable</u>, <u>unprovable</u>, or <u>questionable</u>.

I recently received an e-mail message of _____ truthfulness. Of course,

1.

whether or not it's a good idea to even open these types of forwarded messages is

_____. However, I did open it. According to the e-mail story, a woman and

2.

her daughter had enjoyed a delicious cookie in the café of a high-end department store in the United

States. The cookie was so good that the woman asked for the recipe. The server replied that woman

could purchase the recipe for "two fifty." The woman agreed and asked that the charge be added to

her credit card bill. When the woman received her bill in the mail, the charge for the cookie recipe was

two hundred and fifty dollars—not two dollars and fifty cents. I guess a lot of people must find this

story _____, because the message keeps getting forwarded. Personally, I don't buy the

3.

story. Of course, the story is not completely _____. All you would have to do is go to

4.

the store's café and ask to buy the cookie recipe—and pay in cash.

12 **READING WARM-UP** Have you ever heard a story you thought was questionable or a hoax?
Write the story below. How believable is it? Is it provable?

_____

_____

_____

_____

_____

13 **READING** Read the article.

On the evening of Sunday, October 30, 1938, people listening to their radios in the U.S. received some terrifying news: CBS radio was reporting that explosions had been detected on the planet Mars, and that alien spaceships had landed in New Jersey. The radio announcer reported "live" from the landing site, describing the fearsome creatures that emerged from the ships. Next, the radio reported that the Martians were apparently advancing on New York City, killing anything that came in their path. Soon after, the radio reported that Martian ships had also landed in Chicago, Illinois, and St. Louis, Missouri.

In 1938, radio was a major source of news and entertainment, with people listening to programs for information, just as people often get information from their TV's or computers today. Estimates are that possibly a million people heard the broadcast and panicked, sure that the Earth was under Martian attack. Highways became jammed with traffic as terrified people attempted to escape the areas in which the ships had landed.

In reality, the "reports" were all part of a radio adaptation of a science fiction novel by H.G. Wells titled *War of the Worlds*. The program was performed live on the radio by the Mercury Theater company, headed by actor and director Orson Welles. (Though the names are similar, the author and actor were not related.)

At the beginning of the radio broadcast, Welles announced that the program was a performance of the story, but many people had turned on their radios after the program had already started and missed that announcement. Welles and the other actors used state-of-the-art equipment for sound effects and worked hard to make their program sound like a real radio news broadcast. They succeeded beyond what anyone had expected. Welles was even forced to go back on the air to reassure people that what they had heard was actually fiction.

Welles said later that no one had ever intended to fool the public. In fact, according to some of the actors involved, many people thought that listeners would be bored by the performance or would think it was ridiculous. They couldn't have known that people would think the broadcast was real. Welles himself was afraid that it would be a complete failure. Instead, *War of the Worlds* launched his career, and he went on to be a much-celebrated movie director and actor.

Now answer the questions.

1. What was *War of the Worlds*?

_____

2. What was its effect on people in the U.S.?

_____

3. Do you find it believable that Welles didn't intend to fool people?

_____

4. Imagine you had heard the program. Do you think you could have been fooled? Why or why not?

_____

5. What do you think you would have done if you had believed the broadcast?

_____

LESSON 4

14 **Look back at the article in Exercise 13. Answer the questions.**

1. Do you think CBS radio was to blame for the panic that *War of the Worlds* caused? Explain.

_____

_____

2. What, if anything, do you think the broadcasting company should have done differently?

_____

_____

3. In 1938, people didn't have the Internet to fact-check what they heard on the radio. How else do you think they could have determined if the "news" they were hearing was true?

_____

_____

15 Describe a story that you didn't believe at first, but which turned out to be true, or one that you initially believed, but which turned out to be false. Where did you first hear the story? How did you find out the truth?

_____

_____

_____

_____

_____

GRAMMAR BOOSTER

A Match the questions and answers. Write the letter on the line.

_____ **1.** Did the early inhabitants here grow their own food?

_____ **2.** Do you think the Nazca Lines were carved by aliens?

_____ **3.** Did I write that letter? I can't remember.

_____ **4.** I wonder if the photo of the sea monster was created on a computer.

_____ **5.** Do you think the package came from Jennifer?

_____ **6.** Do you think Steven was fooled by the story?

a. They couldn't have been.

b. It might have.

c. They must have.

d. It must have been.

e. He might have been.

f. You must have.

B Respond to each statement or question with a short response, using the perfect modal in parentheses.

1. A: I wonder if there really was a person named King Arthur.

B: _____ (could)

2. A: Do you think people used water to move the stones?

B: _____ (might)

3. A: Was the newspaper story of aliens in London a hoax?

B: _____ (had to)

4. A: Were the monkeys moved to a different area of the zoo last night?

B: _____ (must)

5. A: Do you think the crew of the *Mary Celeste* was snatched by a giant octopus?

B: _____ (couldn't)

6. A: Do you think Falcon Heene's father knew how upset Falcon would be?

B: _____ (might)

A **PREWRITING: MIND MAP** Think about the time you made a new friend. Recall details of the meeting using the questions on the mind map. Expand each branch as necessary. Use words or sentences. Don't worry about grammar or punctuation.

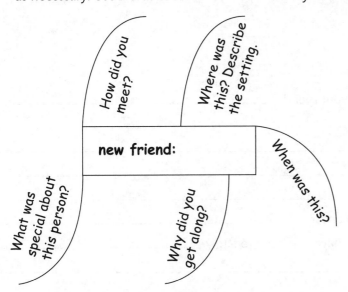

How did you meet?

Where was this? Describe the setting.

new friend:

When was this?

What was special about this person?

Why did you get along?

WRITING MODEL

A New Friend

Last summer I made a new friend while on vacation in Italy. I was hiking in a region called Cinque Terre when I met a man named Flavio. We discovered that we both spoke English, and we began talking. We got along so well that he invited me back to his family's home for lunch. I met his mother, father, and brothers and sisters. His mother made a delicious lunch, and we ate it in their beautiful home overlooking the ocean. I spent a delightful afternoon with Flavio and his family, and by the end of the day we were friends. We still write to each other, and I plan to visit again next year.

B **WRITING** Use the mind map to write about meeting a new friend. Try to include as many interesting details as possible. Choose a title that reflects your main idea. Make sure to avoid sentence fragments.

_____

_____

_____

_____

_____

_____

_____

_____

_____

_____

_____

C **SELF-CHECK**

☐ Do all my sentences express complete thoughts?

☐ Did I avoid sentence fragments?

☐ Did I avoid run-on sentences?

Your Free Time

1 **Answer the questions.**

1. Where do you like to hang out with your friends? _____

2. Where do you go to relax? _____

3. What's your idea of excitement? _____

4. What TV shows do you watch? _____

5. What sports do you play? _____

6. Do you attend sports events? Which ones? _____

7. Do you attend cultural events? What have you been to lately? _____
_____

8. What are your hobbies? _____

2 **WHAT ABOUT YOU?** Complete the survey.

About how much time do you spend on the Internet each day? _____

What do you do on the Internet? Check all the activities you engage in.

- ○ e-mail
- ○ news
- ○ games
- ○ shopping
- ○ banking

- ○ music
- ○ chat/instant messaging
- ○ information searches
- ○ surfing
- ○ other: _____

Do you think you spend too much time online?
_____

If you didn't have Internet access, what would you spend more time doing?
_____
_____
_____

3 **Write the name of a person you know for each category. Provide examples.**

1. Someone who's sociable: _____

2. A loner: _____

3. Someone who's active: _____

4. Someone who's sedentary: _____

5. Someone who's laid back: _____

4 **Answer the questions.**

1. Do you ever feel like you're on call for work or something else? Explain. _____

   _____

2. Do you have a lot on your plate right now? Give examples. _____

   _____

3. Have you ever slacked off on a project or obligation? What happened? _____

   _____

4. Describe a time when you were a nervous wreck. _____

   _____

5. Describe a time when you gave it your all. Was it worth it? _____

   _____

Tips for maintaining work-life balance

1. Don't do work on your commute home. Use the time to unwind.

2. At the end of every work day, write a list of unfinished tasks and when you will complete them. Then stop thinking about them.

3. Exercise after work. It's a great way to reduce stress.

4. Don't check work e-mail once you get home.

5. Schedule time to do nothing. It's okay to just relax!

5 **Give each person some advice. Use phrases from the box.**

learn to laugh things off	set limits	take a breather
set aside some down time	slow down	take up a hobby

I've been working on this report all day without a break. I'm getting a headache.

I've been working so much lately — weekends, too. And when I'm not working, I'm attending class or studying!

1. <u>You really should take a breather now and then.</u>

2. _____

Let's see… I have to finish this report by 12, then I have a quick lunch meeting, then I have to run across town for another meeting, and from there I hope to catch the 5:30 train.

My colleagues have started calling me at home to discuss work. I'm not sure what to do about it.

3. _____

4. _____

Did you hear what Kevin said? He made fun of my tie!

I don't feel like I'm very interesting. All I do is work. Work and eat and sleep.

5. _____

6. _____

6 **Choose the correct word or phrase to complete each sentence.**

1. Ella _____ have a piano lesson tomorrow.

    a. is supposed to   **b.** will be supposed to

2. He _____ park there.

    a. didn't suppose to   **b.** wasn't supposed to

3. _____ turn in our homework yesterday?

   a. Weren't we supposed to   **b.** Aren't we supposed to

4. Where _____ meet the tour group?

   a. we're supposed to   **b.** are we supposed to

5. Is this movie _____ good?

   a. supposed to be   **b.** supposed

7 **Complete the sentences expressing expectations with <u>be supposed to</u>.**

1. (We / arrive at 5:00) _We're supposed to arrive at 5:00_____ tomorrow.

2. (They / not / open their gifts) _____ before we get there.

3. (When / Tina / take a break) _____ and rest? She looks tired.

4. (We / go hiking) _____ yesterday, but it rained.

5. (Who / wash the dishes) _____ last night?

6. (Loretta and Bob / come) _____ to the party later.

7. (Peter / visit) _____ this afternoon? I'll make sure I'm here.

8. (You / not smoke) _____ in here. Would you mind
   going outside?

LESSON 2

8 **Correct the errors in these sentences.**

1. When I was young, I was ride my bike wherever I went.

2. Mario would always building something when he was a kid.

3. We would love being outside all summer long when we were
   younger.

4. My brother used to helping our neighbors shovel snow.

5. In her childhood, Nadia was always play in the snow with her sister.

9 **CHALLENGE Circle the correct words or phrases to complete the paragraph.**

My sister and I had a wonderful childhood. We grew up in the country, and we made the most of it.

There was a special place in the woods where we (1. would play / were always playing) every day.

Lots of wildflowers grew there, and we (2. was always picking / would pick) lots of them to take home.

It seemed like we (3. were always doing / used to do) something outside. We had a dog, and she

(4. used to like / would like) to come with us wherever we went. She (5. used to be running /

was always running) ahead of us, but as soon as we called her, she (6. would come / was always coming)

right back to us. In the winter, we (7. would enjoy / used to enjoy) the outdoors just as much. We

(8. would play / were always playing) in the snow for a while, but then we (9. would end up /

were ending up) having a snowball fight. I have many happy memories of those times.

10 **WHAT ABOUT YOU?** What is a hobby you'd like to try? What do you think you would like about it? What do you need to do to get started?

_____

_____

_____

LESSON **3**

11 How do new technological tools make people's lives easier? How do they take away from leisure time? Name one positive aspect and one negative aspect of each of the technologies listed.

Technology	Positive	Negative
cell phones		
tablets		
laptops		
e-mail		
texting		

12 Read the article on Student's Book page 116 again. Then complete the sentence below in three different ways, using double comparatives.

According to the author, the more we use our devices...

_____ .

_____ .

_____ .

13 Think about your day yesterday. Answer the questions.

1. How many hours did you spend working or studying? _____

2. How much free time did you have? What did you do? _____

_____

3. If you work, did you work after hours? What technological tools did you use to do your work?

_____

4. Did you talk to any friends yesterday? If so, did you see them in person, talk to them on the phone, or send them an e-mail or a text message? _____

_____

_____

. . . Work at Home, Play at Work . . .

Thanks to the Internet and other relatively new technological tools, more and more employees work after hours. They check their e-mail before they go to bed at night, take business calls while out to dinner with friends, and check their text messages at family picnics. Nowadays, if you're sick, you don't have to take a day off. Why waste a day sleeping and watching movies when, with a laptop and an Internet connection, you can work from home? It seems that the line between work and leisure has become blurry and that more technology for work has meant less time for ourselves.

However, technology has not only helped work invade people's leisure time, but it has also allowed people to engage in leisure-time activities at work. With the computer on your office desk, you can leave work virtually. You can check the score of last night's game, do a little shopping, catch up on the news, order concert tickets, plan a vacation, chat with your friends, or just browse the Web. You can appear to be working hard—plugging away at

your computer—when in reality you're reading a fashion magazine online.

According to a recent survey, more than half of the employees questioned said they spent between one and five hours a day surfing the Internet at work for personal reasons. There are even websites dedicated to keeping bored workers amused while they wait for the end of the work day. A psychotherapist who treats Internet addiction explains, "It's like having a TV at everyone's desk. People can watch whatever they want and do whatever they want."

Perhaps a more definite separation of work and home life would be better not only for employees but also for employers. It's not healthy for workers to have access to work 24/7*. And maybe if employees weren't busy working at night and on the weekends, they wouldn't have to e-mail their friends while they're at work.

* 24/7 = 24 hours a day, 7 days a week

Now complete each sentence with a word or phrase from the article.

1. If something is not clear, it's _____.

2. When something unwanted interferes with your time, it _____ your time.

3. If you do something on a computer, rather than in the real world, you do it _____.

4. If you're working hard at something, you're _____ at it.

5. If you do something all the time, you do it _____.

15 **Answer the questions, using information from the article in Exercise 14.**

1. What are some ways people are able to work from home? _____
   _____

2. What are some ways people are able to engage in leisure-time activities at work?
   _____

3. What's the author's point of view in the article? _____
   _____

4. Do you agree with the author's point of view? Why or why not? _____
   _____

16 **WHAT ABOUT YOU?** Look at the list of technological tools below. First, circle the ones you have or use. Then indicate how difficult it would be for you to live without each.

How difficult would it be to live without _____?	not difficult at all	somewhat difficult	extremely difficult
a cell phone	○	○	○
a tablet	○	○	○
a laptop	○	○	○
e-mail	○	○	○
the Internet	○	○	○
texting	○	○	○
a smart watch	○	○	○

According to some estimates, 65 percent of employees go online at work for personal, not work-related purposes every day. Of employees between the ages of 18 and 33, the number goes up to 73 percent.

Of the technological tools listed, which would be the most difficult for you to live without? Why?

_____

_____

LESSON 4

17 Place each of the activities in one of the categories below.

bungee jumping	mountain biking	surfing
extreme skiing	rock climbing	waterfall jumping
hang gliding	skydiving	white water rafting

I've already done it.	I can't wait to try it.	It could be fun.	Not a chance!

18 Take the quiz to see if you have a risk-taking personality.

QUIZ **Are you a risk taker or a risk avoider?**

1 Which type of movie would you rather watch?
a. scary
b. funny

2 Which would you rather do at an amusement park?
a. go on a roller coaster
b. see a show

3 Which sentence describes you better?
a. I love trying new things.
b. I prefer to stick close to home.

4 Which genre of music would you rather listen to?
a. urban dance
b. pop

5 What kind of clothes do you wear? Pick one adjective from each pair.
a. trendy   **a.** flashy   **a.** wild
b. classic   **b.** subdued   **b.** conservative

6 Which do you prefer?
Pick one choice from each pair.
a. to stand out in a crowd   **a.** fast-paced city life
b. to conform   **b.** slower pace of the country or suburbs

7 What are your shopping habits?
a. impulse buying
b. comparison shopping

8 How do you spend your free time?
a. I find something exciting to do.
b. I catch up on work and chores.

9 Which would you rather take up?
a. karate
b. quilting

10 Pick the adjective or phrase that best describes you from each of the following pairs.
a. thrill-seeking   **a.** rebellious   **a.** aggressive   **a.** adventurous
b. conservative   **b.** obedient   **b.** cautious   **b.** prefer routine

a. a troublemaker   **a.** self-confident **a.** energetic   **a.** outgoing
b. well-behaved   **b.** nervous   **b.** calm   **b.** shy

Count up your score.

How many a's did you check? _____

How many b's did you check? _____

0–5 a answers: You probably have a "small t" personality. You don't like thrills and prefer to avoid them. You're among the faint of heart. You prefer certainty and routine. But don't get too set in your ways. A little adventure from time to time would do you some good.

6–11 a answers: You fall somewhere in the middle of the risk-taking continuum. You're probably willing to take some risks from time to time, but maybe prefer to avoid risk in general. Sounds like you live a pretty balanced life.

12–20 a answers: You probably have a "big T" personality. You love thrills and can't get enough of them. You're happiest living on the edge. You like to take risks and do new things. Remember: risk-taking can be the key to success, but it can also get you into trouble. Make an effort to exercise some caution.

How do your quiz results compare with your answer to Exercise E on Student's Book page 119? If they differ, which do you think is more accurate? Explain.

_____

_____

19 Complete each sentence with an adverb of manner. Form adverbs from the adjectives in the box.

beautiful	lucky	quiet	safe
confident	physical	sad	

1. Loraine spoke _____ about her plans for the future.

2. She went skydiving yesterday and landed _____, I'm happy to say.

3. There were no survivors of the plane crash, _____.

4. I fell when I was rock climbing, but _____, I wasn't hurt.

5. Luke sang _____ last night.

6. Checking your devices before bed can affect you _____.

7. Lin walked as _____ as she could, so she wouldn't wake anyone.

> "... it is uninteresting to do easy things. We find out about ourselves
> only when we take risks, when we challenge and question."
> — Magdalena Abakanowicz, Polish artist, born 1930

GRAMMAR BOOSTER

A Rewrite each statement, using <u>be supposed to</u>.

1. Everyone says windsurfing is hard to learn. _____

2. My friends all think that movie is horrible. _____

3. Everyone says the new CEO is a tyrant. _____

4. They say that border collies are extremely intelligent dogs. _____

_____

5. It's said that playing piano makes you better at math. _____

_____

6. I've never been to Hawaii, but everyone says it's beautiful. _____

_____

7. My friends all thought the book was better than the movie, but I thought the movie was better.

_____

B Decide how <u>would</u> is used in each sentence. Write the letter on the line.

a. to express past repeated or habitual actions

b. as the past form of the future with <u>will</u>

c. to express past intentions or plans that changed

d. for polite requests in the present or future

e. to express a present or future result of an unreal condition

_____ **1.** We would just sit and talk for hours when we were younger.

_____ **2.** Jan thought she would become a doctor, but she ended up being a teacher.

_____ **3.** Lauren promised she would pick me up on time.

_____ **4.** Ellie, would you please help me with my homework?

_____ **5.** If Melissa didn't work so hard, she would have more time to relax.

_____ **6.** I wouldn't go skydiving even if you paid me.

_____ **7.** My dad would read stories to us every night.

_____ **8.** Ron said he would read the book on vacation.

_____ **9.** Tania said, "Would you please hurry up?"

_____ **10.** I didn't think I would like that play, but I was wrong. It was great!

_____ **11.** You wouldn't be scared of the water if you knew how to swim.

_____ **12.** Our class would go on a trip together every year.

C Rewrite the sentences using the adverb of manner in parentheses.

1. Monet's paintings are beautiful. (incredibly) _____

2. Ella answered her phone. (angrily) _____

3. Our new employee always works. (hard) _____

4. Bill asked Ty not to smoke. (politely) _____

5. That new sports car is fast. (unbelievably) _____

6. She waved when she saw her friend. (happily) _____

7. She walked away. (slowly) _____

8. David remembered that he needed to call his sister. (suddenly) _____

D Write your own sentences, using the adverbs in parentheses.

1. (well) _____

2. (poorly) _____

3. (suddenly) _____

4. (sadly) _____

5. (slowly) _____

A **PREWRITING: T-CHART** Go back to the article "Work at Home, Play at Work" on page 103. Reread the article and underline sentences that you agree or disagree with. Then write notes on the T-chart. You can quote the author or paraphrase. See the model on the right.

agree	disagree
I agree that technology has allowed people to engage in leisure time activities at work. Many people use the Internet at work for personal reasons. The writer mentions "a definite separation of work and home life." I agree that this is missing in today's world.	I don't think working from home is a bad thing. It is good for employees to have a little flexibility.

agree	disagree

B **WRITING** Write a critique of the article. State your own opinion at the beginning. Then use the notes from your T-chart to support your point of view.

_____

_____

_____

_____

_____

_____

_____

_____

_____

_____

_____

_____

_____

_____

C **SELF-CHECK**

☐ Did I use connecting words and phrases to present and support my opinions?

☐ Did I use quotation marks when citing the writer's own words?

☐ Did I paraphrase the writer's words when I didn't use direct speech?